Secrets of
The
French
Diet

Secrets of
The French Diet

CUISINE FRANÇAISE POUR RESTER MINCE

French Cuisine to Lose Weight

Robert A. Ziff, MD

ISBN 0-9667315-0-6

Library of Congress Catalog Number 98-090855

To my wife, Susan, without whose untiring efforts
this work would not have been possible.

Table of Contents

From left to right: JeanPaul Lacombe, Chef-owner of Léon de Lyon, two stars from Michelin, 18/20 Gault-Millau; Régis Bulot, International President of the prestigious Relais & Chateaux group of Restaurants and Hotels; Michel Troisgros, Co-owner of Troisgros, Roanne, two stars Michelin, 19/20 Gault-Millau; Robert Ziff, author of this book; Pierre Orsi, chef-owner of Orsi, Lyon, one star Michelin, 16/20 Gault-Millau.

Secrets of
The French Diet

CUISINE FRANÇAISE POUR RESTER MINCE
French Cuisine to Lose Weight

At an outdoor café in Marseilles

Imagine that you are sitting in a café in Paris, perhaps on a sunny afternoon, enjoying a tisane, or a Perrier-Menthe. You look around you at the well-worn brass-rimmed tabletop, the woven-backed bistro chairs.... The people chat animatedly around you, some older, some younger, some in couples, some in larger groups, all under the red and white umbrellas that proudly announce a brand of vermouth. You become aware that while people are all different, most of these people are not overweight.

About French Cooking

Why? The French are known to be passionate about food. If ever there were a people whose national heritage is linked to food, it is the French. Did you know that our modern-day restaurants owe their heritage in great part to the French revolution (1789-99)? Prior to that, there were no restaurants as we know them now. Food was served at home, in a small cottage or a big castle, in casserole style dishes or as roasts that were brought to the table and carved. Even at an inn, food was not served on individual plates. That's because you, the customer, couldn't see the whole piece of meat from which your portion came, and therefore didn't know if it was safe to eat. Also, you didn't know who had eaten part of that same roast before you!

The revolution brought an end to the French noble classes, and many of the chefs of these chateaux found themselves out of work. Although some continued to work for the upper classes, many began to open their own establishments where anyone who could pay for a meal could eat like a royal. The idea of à la carte dining was first set out in print by Antonin Carême (1784-1833). Until then, if you ate at an inn, you ate the table d'hôte, which offered little choice. His new book suggested that the guest be offered a list of recommendations from the kitchen. Thus, the tradition of being served a plate of food of your choice off a menu, rather than whatever the innkeeper was making that day for everyone, was born in France at that time.

So there is a long tradition of love of food amongst the French. Certainly no one would argue that some of the most famous chefs in the world have come from France. Pierre François la Varenne (1615-78) authored the first known cookbook, Le Vrai Cuisinier Français, published in 1651, which is still good reading. George Auguste Escoffier (1847-1935) wrote Le Guide Culinaire, a book so profound it is still in use around the world today. He is responsible for organizing the positions of the restaurant kitchen as we know them today. Fernand Point (1897-1955) was chef/owner of La Pyramide, one of the first of the "famous" French restaurants of our time. He was one of the first to question the traditions set forth earlier by Escoffier, and in so doing developed the basis for nouvelle cuisine.

Paul Bocuse at his restaurant (three stars Michelin) with the author and his wife, Susan, Collonges-au-Mont d'Or, France

This change in cooking styles from rigid adherence to old tradition to a more creative approach, was carried on by his disciples, Paul Bocuse (see picture this page), Jean Troisgros, Roger Vergé, and Michel Guerard, all of whom are alive and cooking and teaching today. The chefs of France have spread their cooking around the globe, and many countries today have French restaurants often still manned by chefs born in France.

Intermarriage among the European royal families was not unusual, and along with the alliances of state that these unions formed, came a blending of culture and custom. Princess Catherine of Medici (1519-89), for example, came to France to marry, and brought with her all her chefs from the region of Florence, Italy. The large number of Italian-style dishes in today's typical French cooking, including those called "Florentine", can be traced to this influence. Later, just as pasta became a staple in Italy, so did pâtes (French for pasta) in France-- and we certainly see lots of pasta in French cooking now.

An awakening in this country as to the culinary pleasures of French cooking occurred in the early 1960s primarily due to the influence of television and one individual, Julia Child. Her winning personality and cheerful approach made every housewife feel as though she could turn her kitchen into a French farm kitchen! And, Julia actually did a wonderful job of educating people about French cooking, appropriate to the times. This notion of French cooking as she portrayed it then is still what most of us think of when we think of French cuisine. It wasn't always clear that many of the dishes she prepared were what the French would eat as holiday or Sunday fare, rather than for everyday eating. There is a historical distinction to be made here, too. There was haute cuisine which is what was eaten at royal feasts and special occasions, and then there was cuisine bourgeois, which was everyday fare (this distinction still exists in French cooking). Certainly today, the French do not eat haute cuisine on a daily basis.

Well, what do the French eat every day? How do they keep trim and in shape, when everyone knows French food is high in fat? Why don't they gain weight? We hear that a glass of red wine may prevent heart attacks, but that can't be the secret to weight loss, can it? Can you learn to eat as the French do and actually lose weight while eating French food? All these questions and more will be answered as you read on.

About the author

At market in Antibes

First, I'd like to tell you a little about myself, so you'll know how all this got started. I practice medicine for a living in coastal South Carolina. I have lived here 14 years, but came from New York. I grew up there and while in school, I worked, at first part-time, and then full-time in the restaurant business to help pay expenses. I was a waiter, a cook, a bartender, and then a restaurant manager, after which I taught in the hotel-restaurant department of a community college. In fact, I wasn't sure I wanted to go to medical school at that point, and almost went into the restaurant business as a career. During my seven years in the business, I developed a great appreciation for the miracles that a fine chef could perform with a few raw ingredients. I learned that the principles of French cooking underlie the techniques of cooking in most Western cultures today, and that these basics have been codified for us by the French in books like the ones above, so many years ago.

I maintain an active interest in cooking and the restaurant business today, and have since 1988 been a member of the American Culinary Federation and the American Academy of Chefs. I have taken cooking courses, among other places, at the Peter Kump School in New York, the Cordon Bleu in London, the Innoccenti school in Florence, the Roger Vergé School in Mougins, France, and the Escoffier School at the Ritz in Paris. At medical school, I learned a great deal about diet and nutrition, about physiology and about the effect of food on our bodies. Although many physicians gloss over these areas during school, the were of keen interest to me, and they still are.

I have struggled with my own weight through all those years, and still do, balancing my love of fine food--particularly French food--against the scales.

While I never studied French in school, I have had a sufficiently strong interest that I have learned some of the language in visits, studied from books and tapes, and use computer programs as an aid to translation. It has been very important to me to see and translate from the original French, so that I know I'm getting an accurate renditon when I translate a recipe, rather than an Americanized version. In the process, I have discovered some of the true principles of the eating habits of the thin French, and am now prepared to share them with you.

The "Diet" part of <u>Secrets of The French Diet</u>

Now, why would you want to read about a French diet? Do you also love French food? Do you have a weight problem? Do you also notice that the French are not an obese people?

A diet is defined as the collection of all the foods that any person eats. A normal diet is the collection of all the foods that a particular person eats normally, when not trying to follow a prescribed diet of any kind. Many of the normal diets we in this country follow result in obesity, and in fact, obesity is widespread in our country. Its implications stretch from fashion to medical disease, from cosmetic concerns to chronic illness. Leaving aside the current passion for thinness as a fashion statement, I can say that obesity certainly qualifies as a medical illness, in fact a chronic medical illness, for which there is no easy cure.

There are many, many weight loss diets available (check the shelves of any local bookstore), and when there are a hundred "cures" for any illness, you can be sure that no one of them really works well! Now, a person will lose weight on almost any weight loss diet he or she begins, but the problem arises that each person has over a lifetime developed certain diet habits, both of eating and of exercise, that is both of intake and outgo, that predispose that individual to overweight. Therefore, although weight loss may occur when a person starts a particular weight loss diet, that person has learned little to change his or her lifestyle of eating permanently. Therefore that weight loss comes and goes as quickly as the latest fad diet does.

The only conclusion that we can draw from this is that the only way to permanently lose weight is to permanently change a lifetime's collection of eating habits and exercise habits. Now does it sound more like the nearly impossible task it really is?

Fad diets can't do that. They give you a quick loss program so that if you starve yourself as prescribed, they will allow you to shed a few pounds. So what? What have you accomplished? How have you changed your life so that these pounds won't come zooming back at you as soon as you go off the diet? Do you know anyone who is permanently on the "grapefruit" diet, the Atkins diet, the Scarsdale diet, the Beverly Hills diet, the Myrtle Beach diet, the Pritikin diet, the Jenny Craig diet, the "rice" diet, the Slim-Fast diet, the protein shake diet, or even Weight Watchers?

Obesity is a chronic medical problem that requires lifelong attention to eating habits and activity patterns. Your weight results from a complex interaction of your inherited tendencies, your level of physical activity (notice not just exercise), and how much and what kinds of food make up your normal diet.

Why Worry?

Although some who are overweight view their problem as primarily cosmetic, many others need to be concerned with a real threat to their health[1]. The risks of obesity include, first, an increase in the chance of a premature death. The lowest lifetime mortality rate is actually seen in people who are 10 to 15% below the national average. Adults who are overweight are three times as likely to be hypertensive as those who are not overweight. Overweight adults are 150% more likely to have high cholesterol levels than those who are not. People who are overweight develop diabetes ten times as often as the nonobese. Gallbladder disease goes up 28 to 45 % in the morbidly obese. Osteoarthritis of the knee, hip and back increases with increasing weight. Overweight women suffer increased rates of endometrial, gallbladder, cervical, ovarian and breast cancer. Obesity reduces the capacity of the lungs and can lead to sleep apnea which in turn can be fatal. It can lead to an increase in birth defects, specifically neural tube defects of the newborn, and to decreased fertility. Obesity leads to low self-esteem and negative body image, and the obese often suffer subtle discrimination amongst those who may view them as lazy, shiftless, and lacking in willpower.

Weight loss is the most important thing a person can do, short of drugs, to lower his or her blood pressure. Weight loss leads to declining cholesterol and triglyceride levels, not directly related to the actual percentage of fat in the diet. Oral diabetic medications could be completely eliminated, and insulin discontinued in 82% of people who lost at least 22% of their initial weight in a study reported in the International Journal of Obesity[2]. Weight loss can significantly improve developing osteoarthritis on the weight-bearing joints. Reduction of weight can control pulmonary dysfunction in sleep apnea. Weight loss can restore fertility to many women who suffer hormone imbalances. Finally, weight loss can restore a person's feelings of self-worth and give them a positive body image.

Gimme *drugs*, I wanna lose weight!

Recently, there has been renewed interest in the prescription of the class of drugs known as the anorexiants to promote weight loss. Of course, everyone who is overweight wants to believe that he or she can become svelte by just popping a pill! This group of medications act by affecting the chemicals in the brain that tell you whether or not you're hungry.

It works like this. Science has long established that when a person suffers certain kinds of stress (an extreme example would be parachuting into enemy territory), the body goes into what is called "fight or flight" mode. In response to the stress, the brain produces certain neurotransmitters, which are brain hormones that in this case tell you you're up and alert, and not in the least hungry. These are called sympathomimetic effects, and there are certain medications that can produce the same effect with no need for the stress. There is also a neurotransmitter called serotonin that increases feelings of well-being and satiety, and in essence tells your brain that you feel full. Medications such as phentermine and fenfluramine, used in the Fen-Phen diet, and dexfenfluramine (Redux) all work by increasing these neurotransmitters giving the brain the message that you feel well and are full much earlier in the course of eating than is usual for you. Therefore, while on the medication, you eat less because you're not hungry, and you lose weight.

Sounds great? Well, I guess you don't read the newspapers much. Many of these drugs were prescribed to overweight people by physicians with the foreknowledge that there would be some small risk, but the risk turned out to be much larger than anticipated and, in a number of unfortunate cases, fatal. The problem is twofold. First, there are risks associated with all of these medications. Phentermine, for example, can exacerbate heart disease, fenfluramine and dexfenfluramine can react badly with other drugs. Phentermine with Fenfluoramine can cause a severe heart murmur. All of them can cause depression, and all of them can cause a little-known disease called primary pulmonary hypertension, which has a high mortality rate. The incidence of this disease with over three months of use of these medications varies (arguably) from one in 22,000 people to one in 44,000 people, or more. For these reasons, most of these drugs have been taken off the market.

Secondly, perhaps more importantly for most people, these medications are recommended for only short periods of time. Although obesity is known to be a chronic, log-term problem, none of these medications was even considered safe for more than one year. What happens when you discontinue the medication? Rebound! The body has become adjusted to a higher level of these neurotransmitters, and when these levels drop back to normal, many people find themselves with irresistible and unrelenting hunger. This results in inevitable weight gain, often to levels as high or higher than their original weight.

My experience with diets

I, like many people who struggle with their weight, know more about dieting and eating right than most thin people. Why is it so hard for me and not for them? Why is it that no matter what diet I started, sooner or later I was off the diet? Why did I, after a day, a week, a month, a year, feel a sudden compulsion to eat, and threw the diet to the wind? I'm not talking about just eating, I'm talking about *eating*--a driven, compulsive, out-of-control eating! Was I lazy, shiftless, and condemned to be fat forever? Did I lack the necessary motivation or willpower? No! And neither do you!

You have ten times the willpower of the average thin person, who has not had to deny him or herself like you have. But that, I have found is the very crux of the problem. In her book, How to Become Naturally Thin By Eating More,[3] Jean Antonello hits the nail on the head. She explains that the drive to eat that normally follows a period of dieting is the result of deep-seated survival mechanisms that we as humans have. Our body's drive for survival is so strong that it will eventually override our conscious choices when these choices are interpreted by the body as a threat to our survival.

Everyone gets hungry at times. Have you noticed that when you're overweight and dieting you're not allowed to admit (often even to yourself) that you're hungry? All weight-loss diets prescribe an intake level below the amount a person uses up, in order to lose weight. This results in inevitable hunger, and because you are on a prescribed regimen, you do one of three things. Either, you eat fattening foods and are off the diet, you eat "fat-free" or "diet foods" and you only get hungrier, or you don't eat at all and you develop what Jean Antonello calls excessive hunger.

Your body doesn't understand that you're dieting. It only understands that you are developing excessive hunger, and two things are apt to happen. The first is that in order to conserve resources, it slows your body chemistry down so that you burn up an absolute minimum of what you eat. This is a slowing metabolism, and fights every dieter each step of the way. The more fat-free food you eat, the slower your metabolism gets, the less weight you lose.

The second may take a while to develop. If your excessive hunger develops to a certain point, your body will rebel. It will overcome any willpower you might have, no matter how strong, and cause you to overeat! This is what I call the rebound binge. You go completely out of control, and the weight comes zooming back. You see, it is not a lack of willpower at all, but rather it is the excessive hunger that develops with the wrong kind of dieting that causes these diets to be, in the long run, so unsuccessful. No matter how many bowls, for example, of celery you eat, your body does not interpret that these kinds of foods are going to satisfy its real needs. Now be frank. Did you ever feel satisfied after a bowl of celery?

Quick, how can I lose weight real fast?!

Any diet can make you lose weight really quickly, at the beginning. But very few people can keep the weight off. For every time a person loses weight, there is a 95% chance that the person will regain that weight. The reason is that they've learned nothing from the dieting (they've made no permanent changes in the way they eat or burn up calories), and so whether or not they develop a rebound binge when they go back to their normal diet, the weight comes zooming back.

Now stop for a minute and explain to me why it's so important that you lose weight quickly. Forget that upcoming party! If that's your biggest motivation, it's too short-lived for you to actually get the weight off and keep it off.

It seems to me you have the rest of your life to work on your weight. If you keep on dieting the usual way, your weight will be no different ten years from now—I take that back—your weight will be way up ten years from now!

Think about that weight loss group you may have considered going to, you know, the one where they put you on a scale every week and give a big gold star to the fatty who lost the highest number of pounds that week. What difference does it make how much weight you lose in one week? Where's the fire? The only kind of dieting that will keep the weight off you permanently is one where you lose weight so slowly that you never develop excessive hunger, therefore there is no chance of a rebound binge!

It also should be apparent to you by now that in order to lose weight for good, you've got to find a diet that you can live with for the rest of your life. Therefore the diet must be enticing, appetizing, satisfying, and frankly not so very different from the foods you like best or you will never be able to remain permanently with the new way of eating. Therein lies the secret of the French diet.

The buffet of a lifetime

Imagine that a buffet of all the foods you really love to eat was going to be set in front of you--not for just an hour or a day--but for the rest of your life. The variety in foods, by the way, is endless. Now also imagine that you're told to give up any thoughts of ever dieting again. Just eat to your heart's content. What do you think would happen to your weight? Sure, at the beginning you'd binge like crazy and eat, and your weight would skyrocket. But then what? Sooner or later (it varies depending on how badly you've deprived yourself dieting till this time) you'd get fed up with it all. Not that you'd stop eating, of course not. But food would no longer be an obsession. When your body came to the conclusion that the food would always be available, your excessive hunger would disappear for good and you'd finally know what sensible means.

Well, I agree that the above scenario is not likely to happen because we can't carry the buffet in our back pockets. But it can teach us something. First, we have to convince our bodies by what we eat that we are not subject to starvation, so that slowing of the metabolism and rebound bingeing will not develop. Second, we must provide healthy but not fat-free food in sensible amounts, so that we will both lose weight slowly and not feel in the least deprived. This is a good time to make the point once and for all that the problem with eating a relatively fat-free diet is that doing so results in the body craving fat, overwhelming the willpower, and results in rebound bingeing. Remember, the body will always win a battle between it and your willpower.

The secret then seems to lie in choosing foods that have sufficient nutrients, including fat, that will convince the body that there is no fake famine going on. If you can reduce the amount of the intake just slightly, not greatly, and increase the amount burned up just slightly, you will not have a rebound and you will not be hungry. Since you are not starving the body, it will feel no need to cause you to break out of the diet and binge! It will not interpret your eating patterns as starvation and will not slow your metabolism, and you will lose the weight permanently! Remember, the slower, the better!

Breaking a lifelong habit

Also, it is necessary to remember that the way you are eating now is a lifelong habit. Breaking a lifelong habit doesn't happen overnight. It must be a slow and deliberate process. But people who are fat, especially those who have been on diets before, really have got great willpower. That willpower can be used to your advantage to break those old habits! Allowing yourself to become hungry because of denial, a part of all traditional dieting, has got to be one of the first things to go. The reason for this is that when you become hungry, you overeat.

Think about that. When you sit down to eat in a restaurant, if you're hungry, do you have what my mother used to call "big eyes"? That is, do you order more than you really should eat? How would you order if you had eaten something before you went to the restaurant? Have you ever gone food shopping at the supermarket when you were really hungry? Does your cart get fuller than it should be because everything looked particularly appetizing?

Are you really hungry?

One of the things that you will learn to do as you read on is to decide if it's really hunger you're feeling, or if it's something else. Are you tired? Stressed out? Do you eat when you feel tired or stressed? Remember that the body's natural reaction to stress is the "fight or flight" mechanism. Have you suppressed your own body's mechanisms to the point that when you are stressed you eat (a lot of us have)? You will need to actually think each time if it is really hunger you are feeling.

I remember that when I was a resident in training, I spent many nights awake taking care of patients. I always felt like eating at midnight, at two or three A.M., and again around six. I ate, and ate, and ate! Sometimes I was able to squeeze a nap in there, and on the nights I did so, I didn't eat as much. Think carefully about what your body is telling you when you are hungry ad see if it is really hunger, or if hunger is a substitute for what you are really feeling.

Why a French diet?

Everyone knows—or thinks they know—that French food is fattening, right? Yet the French are not a fat people. Could this be because their food is sufficiently varied, sufficiently nutritious, and has a sufficient fat content to be satisfying? Satisfying enough that a sensation of fullness develops after eating, without overeating? Could it be that French portion sizes are smaller than those typically found in America (forget your traditional notion of our Franco-American restaurants) because the food is sufficiently tasty and filling that more is not necessary?

Do you think that French food is some of the best food in the world, and that you could happily go on eating it (occasionally mixing in other cuisines) for the rest of your life as a lifestyle? Could the secret to breaking the old habits be to start with a cuisine which is inherently delicious, and which you'll look forward to eating so that neither you nor your body thinks you're dieting? I believe you can! I believe that following the tenets of eating as I will set them out for you will be a pleasure, rather than a feeling of denial and mean restriction, and as such, you will enjoy and derive great satisfaction from the dishes you will learn to prepare. I believe that by following this plan, you will not be hungry, but instead will learn to eat moderate portion sizes and feel fulfilled. Since the foods are not fat-free, there will be no pent-up craving for fats, and you will not find yourself longing to go off the diet and developing a rebound binge. A word of caution here. Remember what we said about permanent weight loss. Don't try to do too much too soon or it won't work.

Real French Food:
Cuisine Actuelle

When trying to figure out how the French could possibly eat all that high fat food and remain so thin, my first realization occurred as a result of actually translating some of the recipes I found in French cooking magazines.

A cassoulet like this one from Castelnaudary is a wonderful treat, but at over 1200 calories, can't be everyday fare

PRINCIPLE NUMBER 1:

Much of the food you see in French restaurants, while excellent and appropriate for that special holiday celebration, is not what people eat in France on a day-to-day basis.

The same may be said for a number of French cookbooks that I see on the shelves of our local bookstore. On the other hand, some of the food I see passed off as "French" is so Americanized that you can't ever tell it had French roots (as an extreme example, think of a "Croissant-wich"). This is not the food that I will be suggesting for this way of life, because this is not what people are actually eating on a day-to-day basis in France.

Second, realize that this is not a fad diet, nor will it make you shed "eight pounds a week or your money back". The amount of weight you lose will depend entirely on you, but if you follow closely to what I am going to tell you, you will be eating some of the most delicious food in the world and losing weight! Remember, this is intended as a way of life, not a diet that you stay on for a few weeks with a weight goal. The last thing you want is a fad diet that will make you lose weight quickly. I know that you thought that's what you wanted, and I'm here to tell you *it ain't so*.

What this is intended to be instead is a way to eat. I want you to think of this as a basis for eating, a list of old favorites, from which you can then branch out. This is intended to be everyday food, that won't require hours of preparation, but which can be put together by anyone after a day's work, and yet will result in the most delicious meals you can imagine. Some of these recipes are quite simple, while others have been created by some of the top chefs in France. They are well aware of the problem of overindulgence in food, and guess what? Many of them are not fat!

If you're like me, you'll end up going out to eat less often, because local everyday type restaurants simply can't match the flavors of these foods. And, you can eat without guilt, knowing that none of them is too high in calories for a regular weeknight meal. Sure, you'll go and eat out once in a while, but these dishes are so satisfying that there'll be no sense of denial in coming back to them. You won't end up hungry, because they are truly satisfying, containing enough of that most basic and required substance--fat--to prevent your body from rebelling and going "off the diet," yet little enough to allow you to slowly lose all that excess weight.

According to the National Academy of Sciences in Washington, D.C., millions of people in this country are dieting, and most of those are following quick weight loss programs. Of those that manage to lose 10% of their starting weight, the overwhelming majority will have regained 66% of the weight lost in the first 12 months after the diet, and almost all of it by the five year mark. They approach dieting like a student approaches cramming for a final--lose all you can in this short period so that you get the diet over with, and you can go back to eating "normally" again (they call it *maintenance*).

Fresh market ingredients from Aix-en-Provence

This philosophy is completely backwards! The *normal* mode of eating ought to be one in which you are is slowly losing weight, to allow for those "holiday" times when you gain. Unless you change your way of eating for life, there's no hope! Don't ask, "How much weight can I lose in the next 2 months?" Ask instead, "How much will I weigh 2 years from now?" Or 20 years from now!

The wonderful part of The French Diet is that you'll actually enjoy it. That's the reason it will become a way of life and not a "diet" which you can't wait to quit! For all these reasons, I want you to approach what I'm going to say with a fresh and open mind. It's going to work.

Finally, one of the reasons that this is going to be delicious food is because the raw materials we have in this country are excellent. While it is true that sometimes we have to make substitutions for some of the ingredients found readily in France and not found here, that is no different than

What's fresh at the Forville Market in Cannes, today

what the average French chef does when he goes to market. He looks at what is fresh and decides to use it in his dish instead of what he used when he made the dish the last time. If you have been in French markets like I have, you will know that not everything for sale is fresh. I have seen old, wrinkled potatoes for sale, partly rotten fruit, scrawny chickens, and limp vegetables. Of course, I have also seen magnificent fresh meats and produce that match or beat what's available in the United States. The French cook with what looks fresh because not everything in the market is always edible and appealing, nor is everything always available. Their traditional markets are much more seasonal than our supermarkets are, whereas we tend to fly in a lot of otherwise out-of-season food. Many times that food is picked abroad early enough so that it will not rot on the shelves by the time it gets shipped and distributed here. Picking it that early means that when you buy it, it may look pretty, but it has no taste. That is why it's so important to select a seasonal recipe, and/or substitute with what's best at any given time.

Just as the chefs of France do, you must learn to substitute too, switching for example, the fresh local fish you can get in your area for the fish found locally in the Mediterranean and therefore present in French recipes. I want you to substitute canned peeled tomatoes for fresh ones during the winter, because while winter tomatoes are often tasteless, those picked in summer and canned are okay. In typical French style, then, you will vary the dish to accommodate what you feel is best at that moment from what is available to you. I can't emphasize enough how important it is to try to get the freshest, tastiest raw materials you can find. It does make a big difference!

A word here about another craze, "The Mediterranean Diet." What is a Mediterranean diet? There are 14 different countries that form the shores of the Mediterranean, and therefore 14 different cuisines that all treat food differently. As best I can tell, what you're getting in the "Mediterranean Diet" is a mishmash American diet, take away a little beef and load up on olives, pasta and fish, with a little red wine thrown in. The real Mediterranean diet is heavy in oil, cheese and sausages. You surely can't eat like that and expect to lose weight. Our American version bears little resemblance to what is eaten in any of the countries in that area, and as such creates big questions about how effective it can be in a large, diversified, and sedentary society like ours. Healthier--debatably--but certainly not designed for weight loss, with its high proportion of fat.

Also, the health benefits that are touted for the Mediterranean diet need to be taken in context, remembering that their largest meal is midday, frequently taken with friends and relatives, and often followed by a siesta. It is eaten by a people who on average get a great deal more physical activity than we do because America is the land of labor-saving devices, and because much of their society is an agrarian one where a lot of work is still done the old-fashioned way--by hand. It remains unclear what health benefits remain when their foods are transplanted into our lifestyle.

On the other hand if you have traveled in France as I have you will recall that many of the French in the south include dishes of pasta, risotto or, for example, Osso Bucco, as part of their regular repast. This is in part due to the proximity of their borders, and in part due to the heavy Italian influence in France since Catherine de Medici. We intend to take advantage of that diversity, rather than restricting our diet to what we think of only as rigorously "French".

PRINCIPLE NUMBER 2:
Use an authentic recipe.

That is part of what this book is all about. We don't recommend standard "Franco-American" recipes that are laden with fat and calories, and often devoid of taste. Our recipes have been created by the finest chefs of France, those that have won some of France's highest accolades for their cooking. Many of you are familiar with the green and red Michelin Guides, which are

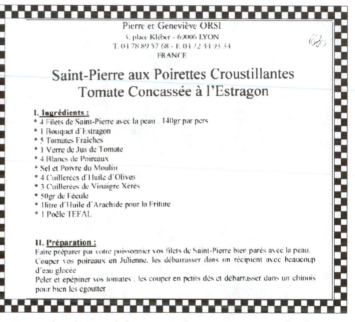

Example of one of the original recipes I've used, this one sent to me by Pierre Orsi, Lyon, France

guide books written to all parts of France (and elsewhere). You also probably know that each restaurant and hotel listed has been carefully reviewed by a Michelin reviewer, and that the top honors go to those who have won "stars" for their cooking. Michelin has issued these ratings for nearly a century, and they are highly respected around the world. Three stars, the highest award, goes to restaurants that serve "exceptional cuisine, worth a special journey." Two stars goes to chefs who provide "excellent cooking, worth a detour." One star goes to a restaurant considered "very good in its category." The great majority of restaurants do not receive any stars. It is a tremendous honor for a chef to be awarded a star, and chefs toil many years before ever hoping to reach that level. Once there, it requires meticulous attention to detail and much hard work to keep that star.

Some of the recipes you will see here have been written by chefs who have won two or three Michelin stars, clearly making them amongst the best in all of France. Some of the other recipes have been written by other French chefs whom I feel are outstanding, and each recipe has been translated by me from the original French, adapting them only so far as necessary to permit them to be cooked in an American kitchen. You may wonder what I mean by that. French recipes are written for kitchens where the stove is calibrated in centigrade, where the liquid measure is in "wineglassesful" or "mustard pots full" or in liters. Dry ingredients are usually weighed out in grams on a kitchen scale. Each of these must be adapted so you will know what is meant. And finally, some of the recipes have been written by me with the guidance and inspiration of these fine chefs, trying to maintain the taste of certain well known dishes while allowing you to enjoy them and still lose weight.

For those of you that understand French, I strongly recommend that you contact some of the sources I have listed in the footnotes, and get some of the original recipes, as you will enjoy cooking from the original French as much as I have. One difficulty in translation is that regular French-English dictionaries are sadly lacking in food terms, and so a French-English food dictionary is a great help. A number of French magazines now have a section for slimmed-down versions of traditional recipes, and I suggest that you may wish to subscribe to one or more of them. Some of their recipes are truly great!

PRINCIPLE NUMBER 3:

The amount you weigh is a direct result of the number of calories you burn up subtracted from the number of calories you eat.

Let's face it, it's that simple. That's why there's absolutely no magic in fat-free diets. It's simply that if they contain fewer calories than your present diet, you'll lose weight. Since, ounce for ounce, fat contains the highest number of calories, a fat free diet appears to work.

One question frequently asked is, "Is it true that calorie for calorie, fat will put more weight on me than carbohydrate or protein?" The answer is that technically yes, it's true, but only by a factor of about two-tenths. The reason is straightforward: when the body absorbs protein and carbohydrate calories in excess, and converts them to fat, it uses up about twenty percent of those calories in energy to accomplish the conversion. When it takes in fat calories in excess, the fat is stored directly without loss. Therefore, fat free is the way to go if you want a crash diet.

However, this fails to take into account some very important variables, such as: how long can you actually stay on such a diet? Or do you find yourself off of it after a few weeks or months because the food is intolerable and there no feeling of satiety? Do you get tired of eating typical fat-free tasteless dishes? Do they leave you feeling as deprived and frustrated as they do me?

Abstinence in dieting doesn't work in the long run. All that happens is that you develop cravings for the foods that you have cut from your diet. With all those fat-free diets, the craving is for that great taste and feeling of satiety that fat-containing foods give you. You end up with rebound bingeing, and your weight goes yo-yoing back up. That, in a nutshell, is the problem with fat-free diets.

PRINCIPLE NUMBER 4:

Chemical diets don't work.

You've seen all the ads for them...they say things like, "Eat this magic combination of foods and the fat will melt away!" or, "The chemical reaction produced by eating these special foods together will cause your weight to plummet!" It sounds good, and is music to the ears of anyone who has tried to lose weight by a real method, but the pure and simple fact is that there is no chemical combination of foods that will make you lose weight.

Other things that don't work might just as well be dealt with right now. Fat burners, and vitamin combinations that burn the fat right off of you are a complete waste of money, unless you want some very high priced vitamins that will do nothing to make you lose weight. Too bad they don't, though....

Plastic sweat suits that sweat the weight right off (and other magic devices) will, at best, cause you to temporarily lose a few pounds on the scale. This is some of that vital water you've been drinking. So, there you are, dehydrated. What do you think the body is going to do? The very next thing that you eat or drink will be hoarded by the body, until it makes up the water loss! Presto, the weight is back. Additionally, you may suffer the effects of dehydration, which I'll come back to later.

"Use this special exercise device and in 20 days you will have washboard abs," the ads proclaim. Ever see a guy with washboard abs and fat every where else? Spot reduction simply doesn't exist. Sit-ups exercise the wrong muscle group; no one exercise will do it. An Adonis body requires a total workout program, and an individual committed to it. Abstain for a while and the flab comes back--fast!

The right answer here for most of us is moderation. We don't want to spend a tremendous portion of our lives doing nothing but exercising, and we won't have a perfect body. What counts is how many calories go in, and how many go out. Exercise in moderation, eat the way I suggest, and you'll look and feel pretty darn good!

PRINCIPLE NUMBER 5:

The largest number of calories burned every day for each of us is used just to keep us alive and functioning in the activities of daily living. Increase your basic activity level, and you lose weight.

There is little black magic in dieting. If you're going to consume fat in a moderate amount in your diet, you have got to figure out a way to get some of it burned up.

Consider that America is the land of labor-saving devices. I should generalize that to labor saving arrangements as well! You don't even have to get out of your car to eat--you just pull right up to the window and the food is handed to you right there in the car! Unheard of in France! If you think about your activities of daily living, you will find dozens of ways that we in this country have developed to save the expenditure of a few more calories of energy. From electric can openers to paper plates to computer banking, we are in the business of trying to make everything easier so that fewer calories are expended in the process. Add it all up and you've got a few hundred calories a day! If because of a new labor-saving device or arrangement you expend just one hundred calories of energy a day less, you'll gain over ten pounds in a year. Inside of a few years, you'll be on one of those fat-free diets trying desperately to get the weight off!

Here's what to do about it:

I want you to think about what you do on a day-by-day, hour-by-hour basis, and go the extra step each time to do it the harder way--perhaps the old-fashioned way--rather than the easy way. Inefficiency is what we're striving for here! As an example, take a short walk before lunch each day--say ten or fifteen minutes. If you eat out at a nearby restaurant, walk there and back. Instead of carrying the laundry up the stairs all at once, make several trips. Do your housework to an aerobics tape (or a Mozart tape for that matter if you like it better), and turn the work into a workout.

You see, the converse of what I said above is true, as well. If you expend just 100 calories of energy per day by walking to the mailbox and climbing the stairs rather than using the elevator, you'll lose over ten pounds in a year!

So, starting right now, I want you to be thinking all the time, how can I expend a little more energy with this chore, how can I do this in a slightly less efficient way, and expend more calories in the process!

That dastardly "exercise" word,

You'll notice I haven't even talked about health clubs, running, or treadmills yet. But the French are a fairly athletic people, and many enjoy aero- bics, "musculation", and other sports activities especially bicy- cling. When you think of a small village in the countryside of France, don't you think of women bicycling to market, and men bicycling on their way to work? Can't you just picture *madame* bicycling home in the early morning from the *boulangerie* with that baguette on the back of her bicycle, going home to a family to enjoy at breakfast? Look how much exercise that provides, just in the routine of life. Think of the most famous bicycle race of them all, the Tour de France!

If you already exercise, no more need be said about it to you. Consider bicycling to work or to market if that is reasonable where you live. Impossible? Then find something you like to do, even if it is just walking twenty minutes a day (which is an excellent habit since you'll be able to do that most of the rest of your life, long after the others have given up racquetball). Don't try to get by with that lame excuse about "no time". There's time for what's important to you. Did you know the average American adult watches 3 to 4 hours of television a day! Not only does being a couch potato burn fewer calories than almost anything else, it encourages snacking in front of the boob tube. You've got one life--make the most of it. Take a portion of that time and devote it to some kind of exercise. Try combining exercise with the TV (see below). I watch TV infrequently, but I enjoy what I watch. I not infrequently tape shows I want to see, so that I zip through the commercials and cut down the amount of time it takes to see a particular show. More importantly, this allows you to see a show when you want to, not when the network says you may. You can tape your favorite shows, and set up an exercise area in front of the VCR.

Here's what to do about it:

Starting today, I want you to find any sort of calorie-burning exercise that you enjoy, and that you can do for twenty to thirty minutes a day. More is not required!

Your objection may go something like this: "If an hour of bicycling won't burn up the calories in a single slice of pie, what's thirty minutes of exercise going to do?"

PRINCIPLE NUMBER 6:
Even as little as twenty to thirty minutes of exercise a day will increase the RATE at which you burn calories all day, and in so doing you'll lose more weight.

The benefits of this extra exertion are going to magnified, and here's why:

It's true that bicycling for an hour only burns up about 425 calories, but the secret lies in what that amount of exercise will do for your overall metabolic rate, when made a part of your regular daily activity. When you start exercising on a regular basis at least three times per week, your metabolic rate is going to go up! That means not only will you lose the calories you burned doing the exercise, but your body will burn more calories in everything you do all day long.

My schedule is hectic, and I refuse to get up any earlier in the morning to go to the gym, since many nights my sleep is already cut short by calls to go to the hospital to take care of patients. In the evening, I work late enough many nights that if I went to the gym, changed, exercised, showered, changed back again, and drove home, I'd probably be starting dinner at ten o'clock! So instead, I have a ski machine set up in front of a TV set. While I'm at work, the VCR records some of those terrific international food programs from NPR, the Food channel, or the Discovery Channel. When I get home, I can exercise for 30 minutes while watching, without all the getting ready and getting unready part. I can do it in the comfort and privacy of my own home, at my own pace.

Being able to watch these programs is, for me, a reward I give myself for exercising, and to keep it that way I don't allow myself to watch them at other times. See the principle here? My system may not work for you, but if you think about it you can set up a reward system for yourself *other* than food which will make the exercise more enjoyable. I have at times found myself so engrossed in what was going on with the TV program, I had long passed my thirty minute goal!

Remember that old saying, "today is the first day of the rest of your life." I know it's hard to change the habits of a lifetime, but today is the day to begin!

PRINCIPLE NUMBER 7:
Increase your muscle mass, and you'll lose even more weight!

Cells of all types in our body are in constant need of calories to keep them going, but the number of calories they require depends on the kind of cell. Fat cells are in the business of storing energy, but they use very little of that energy to do so, and it takes little energy for them to thrive on a daily basis. Muscle cells are the body's engine, and burn calories at a rapid rate compared to fat cells, just in the activities of daily living. Therefore, the larger muscle mass your body has, the more calories it will burn up in any given day just because you're alive!

Think of it this way: A small Renault can make thirty miles on a gallon of gasoline, but a Ferrari will burn more than twice that amount to make the same thirty mile trip. You want to be the Ferrari!

Therefore, a third way in which that exercise is going to help is it's going to increase your muscle mass. And that, in turn, is going to further increase the number of calories you burn up in the activities of daily living.

What's wrong with calorie charts is that they only show the number of calories you burn for doing a specific exercise for a specific number of minutes. They don't show you the number of extra calories you will burn all day because of one, increasing your metabolic rate, and two, increasing your muscle mass.

A Word About Health

Why are you reading this report? Are you concerned about excess weight because it's not fashionable to be overweight? Do your clothes no longer fit? Have you decided that it's expensive to keep replacing your wardrobe with larger sizes? Are you having a self-image problem? Are you concerned that you are less sexually appealing?

Or has the doctor told you to lose weight? Is your blood cholesterol over 200? Are you concerned about heart disease? Certainly many of these may be true for each of you, and it may be a concern to you that as a physician I am not recommending a diet which is necessarily lowfat, since that's all the craze right now. Many of you have learned that Dr. Dean Ornish, eminent cardiologist, recommends an extremely restricted diet of no more than 10% fat. Why is that not the approach to follow?

Well, everyone is entitled to his opinion, and I don't disagree with Dr. Ornish's recommendation, but I can't live that way and I expect a number of you can't either. Nor am I convinced that it's the only way. If going on his type of nearly fat-free diet affects you the way it does me, the next thing that happens is that you're off the diet and eating all the forbidden foods (the rebound binge). The yo-yoing is worse than anything for your body!

When the studies were done that showed that people living in the entire Mediterranean area had low levels of heart disease, it was also shown that they did not have fat intake levels anywhere near as low as Dr. Ornish suggests for us. In fact, their intake of fat, (for example on Crete, where some of these studies were done) showed dietary fat intake in some individuals approaching 40% of total calories. How do we explain this apparent paradox?

It has been known for a the last thirty years or so that heart disease is related to blood cholesterol levels. Since cholesterol is an ingredient in animal fat, doesn't that mean we should restrict our intake of all dietary fats, as Dr. Ornish suggests, to reduce our chances of heart disease?

No, it doesn't, and here's why:
To leap from the knowledge that high blood levels of cholesterol are bad to the idea that all dietary fat is bad, is a leap based on a false assumption. The false assumption is that eating fat raises one's cholesterol levels. It simply isn't true. Only saturated fats raise your cholesterol levels. So there is no medical reason for most people to limit their intake to anything like 10% fat in their diet.

If health and heart disease are a concern for you, forget the amount of total fat in your diet, and limit your intake of saturated fats! Within the parameters I am going to suggest, simply choose those foods that are lowest in saturated fats, and substitute unsaturated fat for saturated every chance you get.

Telling one from the other is not difficult; there are a few rules and a few exceptions. Saturated fats are generally solid, and from animals. Unsaturated fats are generally liquid, and from plants. Two notable exceptions are coconut oil and palm oil which are high in saturated fat, but neither of those are popular in French cooking.

Margarine started out in life as lower in saturated fat because it's made from vegetable oil, but in order to get it to solidify so that it would look and act like butter, they had to hydrogenate its bonds. Hydrogenated unsaturated fat is practically no better for you than if you ate butter, and margarine has the same calorie content as butter. So if you have a particular problem with high cholesterol, choose olive oil over butter, and vegetable oil over bacon fat. If you don't, remember that all oils and fats have just about the same calorie count—that's right—butter and margarine have the same number of calories! So, use in moderation whatever works best in a given dish!

Dieting 101

Step one: buy a pocket calculator and a paperback calorie chart.

The next step is to figure out about what your caloric intake is now. Very simple. Keep a diet diary for about 5 days. Write down everything you eat when you are eating whatever is your normal diet. Don't try to do this retrospectively, you will never remember all the stuff you weren't supposed to be eating but did, and it won't be a true reflection of your caloric intake! Specifically make no effort to curb your intake over these days, or your readings will be inaccurate and mess you up.

Now, get hold of a calorie list from the bookstore, the grocery store, the library—they're available everywhere—and total up the number of calories you ate in these five days, then divide by 5. This will give you the average number of calories you ate per day. Make sure you prepare this diary while you're actually overeating, whichever way you do (everybody's binges are different). If you do it while you're eating the way you think you're supposed to, it will do you no good.

The next step is deciding how overweight you are. Let's try to figure it out scientifically, the French way. The French use a formula to figure out what a person should weigh, based on their height in centimeters, and this gives a result in kilograms. I'm going to help you to convert the formula so that it works in inches and pounds. Use a pocket calculator to do the arithmetic. To begin, figure out your height in inches and multiply by 2.54 cm/in to get centimeters (use that calculator!). Then, rewrite the formula below with your height filled in, in centimeters. Do the arithmetic, and multiply the result in kilograms by 2.2 to get pounds. Voilá, there's your ideal weight.

The following formula is from <u>Maigrir</u> [4]

Men:
$$\frac{(\text{Height in cm.} - 100) - (\text{height in cm} - 150)}{4}$$

Women:
$$\frac{(\text{Height in cm.} - 100) - (\text{height in cm.} - 150)}{2.5}$$

Now, let's go through this one time to show you how it works. I'm 5'8", which is 68". 68 in x 2.54 cm/in rounds off to 173 cm. Following the formula, 173-100 is 73, fill that in. Next, 173-150 is 23, *then* divide 23 by 4 to get 5.75. Plug in that value. Finally, 73 less 5.75 is 67.25, my ideal weight in kg. Then, multiply 67.25 by 2.2 and you'll get about 148 pounds, my ideal weight.

Of course, this doesn't account for bone structure, and needs to be modified if you have a large or small frame. To determine what size frame you have, wrap your fingers around your wrist and see if your thumb meets your longest finger. If they just about meet, you have an average frame. If they overlap, you have a small frame. If your thumb doesn't come near meeting your longest finger, you have a large frame. Add 10% to the above calculation for a large frame, and subtract 10% for a small frame (this method of figuring frame size is not completely reliable, but works fairly well).

A modification can be made for age as well, but there is some disagreement amongst professionals, at least in this country, about whether one ought to weigh more as one ages or not. The French add 2.2 lbs. (1 kg.) per ten years of age starting with age 20. For women, they also add 2.2 pounds for every child born.

Once you have calculated your ideal weight, the next step is to calculate the calorie intake that, at your current metabolic rate, would keep your weight at its present level. This is what we will call your set point. Choose from the scenarios below to help decide which factor to use:

Scenario 1: I walk at a normal rate, I sit at the computer, I drive, I do light office or light housework, I may play golf.

Light activity level =12-14

Scenario 2: I walk at least 20 minutes at a brisk pace at least three times a week; I do heavy housework, yard work, or office work often; I play tennis or racquetball once a week.

Medium activity level = 15-16

Scenario 3: I swim, I jog or walk briskly more than 30 minutes four times or more per week, I play tennis at least twice a week, I do heavy yard work for a living or am a manual laborer.

High activity level = 17--20 (or higher)

Now, choose the scenario that best fits your current lifestyle (leaving out the exercise you mean to do but haven't started regularly yet). Choose a number from within the range given that you feel best describes your current activity level (higher numbers of course mean more activity within each category). Be realistic. Multiply that activity level factor times your current weight in pounds.

For example, if you are in the medium activity level (and chose activity level 15), and you weigh 160 pounds, multiply 160 x 15 = 2400 calories. This is the number of calories required per day to maintain your present weight. However, your actual caloric requirement may be slightly higher or lower, depending for example, on your age. In general, younger people have a higher metabolic rate, which slows with age. The degree to which it slows is partly genetically inherited, partly controlled by exercise, and other factors. Therefore you may need to alter this calculation slightly, especially if you are experienced at dieting and know what results you get at particular calorie levels. If you are not, start with this number as a good base.

Compare this number with the number you reached when you made out your diet diary. They should be somewhat similar. If not, it just shows that either you were unrealistic in your diary, or that your eating habits are so high in calories that your weight won't stabilize--it will just keep on climbing! Take the lower of the two figures, as long as it's realistic.

Now, a decision must be reached about how much to lower the caloric intake per day in order to lose weight. For these purposes we are going to ignore any bonus in caloric expenditure secondary to increased activity and increased metabolic rate. Remember, I don't recommend a drastic reduction in calories for any length of time, because that's not a diet you'll stick with, but you need to lower the caloric intake enough to do two things. The first is to lower it enough to actually lose weight. The second is to lower it a little further to allow an intentional diet holiday for those times when it's necessary to go over the "budget" of calories.

After all, this is intended as a way of life! A Sunday meal with family at a relative's house, a romantic weekend getaway at a hotel, or a special treat that someone made just for you is going to upset your diet, no matter how careful you are at those times. Let's plan for this to happen ahead of time, and accept that as long as it doesn't happen so often your weight is going nowhere, it's perfectly okay, and even to be encouraged.

The reasons I think that it's important to take a diet holiday are, first, psychological, and second, physiological. The psychological reason you might need to go on a short holiday from your diet is so obvious it needs no further clarification, especially to anyone who has ever been on a diet before (tried them all, have you?). The physiological reason may not be so clear.

PRINCIPLE NUMBER 8:

Take a short holiday from the diet plan periodically to prevent your body from going into "starvation mode" and your metabolism from slowing down.

If your body gets accustomed to a certain reduced caloric intake level, it will go into what I call "starvation mode", and actually slow down your metabolism regardless of your activity level. This is the body's natural defense mechanism against starvation, leftover from caveman days. To avoid that, follow what thin French people do naturally and take a short (one meal, one day) holiday. That doesn't mean go wild! And be very sure to get back to the plan immediately after that short holiday. In spite of how important it is to break the routine periodically, I am hesitant to share this secret with you because there is tremendous temptation to throw in the towel after a diet holiday, so you must be especially vigilant about this. Remember this section later when we talk about cravings and psychological hunger.

Author's friend Dru on a diet holiday in Cannes

Now let's get back to deciding on just how many calories you want to eat each day. Don't set your caloric intake below 1200 calories for any length of time unless you are of very small stature and involuntarily sedentary (read wheelchair). Doing so may cause a shift into starvation mode, and you will not see results. Your body will simply become more efficient and burn up fewer calories each day. Now be careful. This only happens if you take in fewer than 1200 calories for a long period of time. So, although it is okay and you in fact may want to kickstart your diet with a very low intake level for a short period of time, just don't stay at that level.

Here's how to set your caloric level for weight loss:

I want you to set your caloric intake for the standard part of the diet (not the beginning...see later) at one of the following preset levels: 1200, 1500 or 1800 calories. The level you choose should depend on your set point, calculated above, what you can reasonably live with, and what your diet diary showed your previous levels to be, and how much weight you need to lose.

Women should generally choose either 1200 or 1500 calories, men 1500 or 1800 calories. If your set point is much higher than 2300-2500 calories, you will have to add to the diet so that you don't lose too quickly. It is reasonable to figure that for each 500 calories a day your caloric intake falls below the set point, you will lose about a pound a week. This is because a pound is roughly 3500 calories, and a 500 calorie a day loss times seven days in a week equals 3500 calories, or one pound.

Now, don't get the idea that you will lose a nice, even one pound a week on a 500 calorie drop. There are other factors we will discuss later such as water weight shifts, plateaus, and metabolic rate change all of which will influence the rate at which you lose. However, if you stuck with it over the long run, just a 500 calorie a day change while following the recipes contained in this report, will result in over a 50 pound weight loss in a twelve month period, and much more for some people. More about that later.

I don't recommend that you try to lose more than one to a maximum of two pounds a week, because you will either shift into "starvation mode", or even if your body doesn't, you will likely not stick with such a radical diet long enough to make a difference. Worse, since it's taught you nothing about how to eat, you'll be back to your regular habits in no time after the "diet" is over, and be rebound bingeing right back up where you started. As I previously said, yo-yoing weight up and down like that can be worse for your health than not losing it in the first place.

Let me make an important point here. We all know that thin French people don't count calories. They don't need to because their set point is adjusted lower than ours. They understand what reasonable means, and we don't. They don't rebound binge.

Because they've been eating that way all their lives, they feel "full" sooner than we do, and simply don't eat any more. They already know what and how much to eat intuitively, while we have to learn this from this scratch. The point of calorie calculations and recipe selection from alimentary groups is so that you can learn to develop your intuition about how much and what to eat at each meal. You need to get back in touch with what your body tells you about when it is full. I don't actually calculate it for every meal any more, though I sure did to start. I still do calculate it periodically. When I look at a piece of chicken or a sandwich, I now know how much of it I should eat. I now pay attention to what my body is telling me, and when I feel full I stop eating. It's very important to realize that you don't need to eat enough so that you're sure you'll be able to make it to the next meal. That's overeating. You need to eat enough so that you're no longer hungry now, and that's it! Remember you can always eat again. They didn't take all the food off the planet just because you quit eating lunch. As you develop your meal plans and get in the habit of the new recipes, you will begin to know how much to serve and/or eat without counting calories each time. How to *stop* at that point when eating out is also later in this report. Just keep on reading....

PRINCIPLE NUMBER 9:

People are overweight because their appestat is adjusted to a level higher than their set point, because they eat too fast, and because they've learned to ignore the signal that they are no longer hungry.

What's an "appestat"? This is a term I use to describe the internal mechanism that tells us we are full. It is supposed to act like a thermostat. A thermostat automatically shuts off the heat when the room temperature comes up to the set point. The appestat is supposed to tell you that you are no longer hungry when you've eaten enough to reach your set point, the point at which calorie intake equals calories burned. If you've been overeating, your appestat is set too high, and you're going to overeat. It resets naturally when you start to eat more reasonably, as this diet is geared to make you do. Even if your appestat is set at an appropriate level, if you eat too fast, the food won't reach your stomach quickly enough to let you know you've eaten enough. By the time it does, you've overeaten!

PRINCIPLE NUMBER 10:

Take a minimum of twenty minutes to eat your main dish, longer if at all possible!

It takes twenty minutes for the food you swallow now to reach the stomach. If you consume an entire plate of food in less than 20 minutes, you haven't even given your body a chance to tell you it's full! The when the food hits your stomach, you realize too late that you've eaten too much. The appestat works, but you've eaten so fast you haven't given it a chance.

That's why it's so important to eat in courses, especially at dinner when your largest calorie intake occurs. That soupe à la tomate appetizer isn't just in the way of your getting down to dinner, it's intended to slow down your eating so that time passes and you get filled up before you've wolfed down more than you're actually hungry for.

If you eat at a normal pace and "subconsciously" realize you're no longer hungry in the middle of eating, but keep on eating, you've trained yourself to ignore what you appestat tells you.

Here's what to do about it:

You must learn to eat more slowly. This is absolutely key, beyond almost everything! You've got to allow time for your appestat to warn you. If you find yourself eating too quickly, stop. Rest. Wait. Resume eating several minutes later.

You must learn to pay attention to when you are no longer hungry. This requires concentration on eating, not on the talk at the table, or your newspaper, or the TV set. Evaluate after each bite, I am I really hungry? Do I really need more of this, or am I just swallowing it down?

You must follow the program of calorie apportionment and meal allocation until, with time, your appestat is reset and then you will just stop eating when you are full! Follow the program and there will come a time when you won't miss more to eat!

Now, here's the part where the science of it gets tricky, and, quite frankly, usually falls apart. We want to allocate an appropriate percentage of the total calorie count for each meal, then further subdivide each meal into allocations for carbohydrate, proteins and fat. Then, we've got to choose foods that fit each of those categories, and combine them into recipes and then meals that are actually edible. You will see why fat-free diets make it easier to eat more volume on a set number of calories, but you also know what they taste like. We're going to be making suggestions that fit the categories reasonably, not always perfectly. Nevertheless, you're going to want to follow them, because they make sense and are going to be enjoyable.

Here's how we do it:
Step one is to learn all you can about the basic food categories: carbohydrates, proteins and fats, and the energy (read calories) they provide.

I know this next section is apt to bore some of you, but I want you to read it anyway. It's important to have at least a basic knowledge of the science of nutrition before you can intelligently decide how to create a balanced diet, especially if you're going to be limiting your variety and intake.

The Basics of Nutrition

All foods can be divided into six basic components, which are: proteins, fats, carbohydrates, vitamins, minerals and water. Water often makes up the largest component of any food substance, and is essential to the chemical reactions that take place in our bodies. Vitamins and minerals are also essential to the body for its chemical reactions, known collectively as the metabolism. Energy is derived by the body during chemical reactions that involve the breakdown of carbohydrates, proteins and fats. Energy is measured in calories (technically Calories, where the capital C stands for the kilo in kilocalories, which is what they are called in Europe). The amount of energy that any food substance provides can be referred to as its calorie count

CARBOHYDRATES

These are the components of food that provide for the immediate energy needs of the body. Foods that are rich in carbohydrates are often colloquially said to be carbohydrates, but even potatoes (a quintessential carbohydrate food) contain small amounts of other nutrients. Carbohydrates are divided into simple sugars or complex carbohydrates. The simple sugars are the quickest form of energy for the body, but the complex carbohydrates require breakdown by the body to be used. Examples of simple sugars are the naturally occurring sugars in milk (lactose), fruit (fructose), and refined table sugar (sucrose). Complex carbohydrates include the starches, such as those found in cereals and potatoes. Fiber, which is actually the structural framework of plants (what bones are to animals), is very important in our diet. Insoluble fiber, such as cellulose, aids in our digestion. Soluble fiber, such as pectin, may help in the immune system, fight cancer, and help control blood sugar levels. The American diet is sadly lacking in fiber, especially insoluble fiber, resulting in shelf after shelf of constipation remedies at our local drugstores.

Current recommendations in both France and the United States are that 55 to 60% of our diet should be made up of carbohydrates. Most of these should be complex carbohydrates, rather than sugars. The body can convert simple sugar to carbohydrate, and does so when sugars are present in the diet in excess of current need. When demand exceeds availability in the diet, they are converted back again. One gram of carbohydrate provides 4 calories of energy.

PROTEINS

Proteins can be further subdivided into animal or vegetable proteins. Foods of animal origin have a higher content of protein (12-30 g/100g) than foods of vegetable origin (3-12g/100g) with the exception of soy which is very high in protein. Proteins are broken down by the body into their component parts, which are the amino acids. There are 22 amino acids in all. Our bodies can rearrange the molecules in amino acids such that we can make 14 of them from the others, but there are 8 that must be in the diet as we cannot make them. These are called the essential amino acids. Animal proteins are called complete proteins because they contain all 8 of these, but vegetable proteins are called incomplete proteins as they do not. True vegetarians can get all 8 by eating a varied diet.

French authorities think that 12 to 15% of each day's calorie intake should be from protein, the newest FDA recommendations here are for 10% protein. One gram of protein provides 4 calories of energy, same as carbohydrates.

FATS

Fats are distinguished from oils in that they are usually solid at room temperature; fats are usually of animal origin whereas oils are usually from plants. Two exceptions are coconut and palm oil, which are solids but are from plants. Fats are broken down into three categories: saturated, mono-unsaturated, and poly-unsaturated. The harder a food belonging to the fat group is, the more likely it is to be saturated (butter is a saturated fat, olive oil is not). The more saturated a fat is, generally speaking, the more unhealthy it is. Cholesterol is a breakdown product of saturated fat. Mono-unsaturated fats are from fish and plants, such as avocados, olives, and nuts. Poly-unsaturated fats are mostly from plants, such as corn, safflowers and soybeans. Mono- and poly-unstaurated fats either have no effect on cholesterol, or tend to lower the harmful portions of it.

Fatty acids, breakdown products of fats, are essential to the body and cannot be made from other nutrients. Fats play an important role in our ability to absorb the fat-soluble vitamins A,D,E and K. U.S. and French authorities both suggest about 30 to 35% of the day's calories should come from fats. Fats are long term storage for the body, and excess complex carbohydrates are eventually converted to fats if the body determines that there are sufficient amounts of calories freely available in the diet. When the diet is low in calories, the body breaks down the fats for energy, but the rate at which it does so is dependent on numerous other factors such as the metabolic rate.

One gram of fat provides 9 calories of energy. Take careful note that this is more than twice the amount of calories from an equivalent amount by weight of either proteins or carbohydrates.

ALCOHOL

Alcohol fits in none of the above categories well. Traditionally, it was said to provide 7 calories per gram of energy, that is, a little more than twice as many per unit of weight as carbohydrates or protein, and almost as many as fat. These were described as "empty calories" thought to be devoid of nutritional value. Now all of this advice is called into question, as scientists begin looking a little harder at alcohol. Recently, researchers at the American Cancer Society found that two glasses of wine a day for men, and one for women, resulted in no weight gain and sometimes even a slight weight loss, in a ten-year study of almost 80,000 people. Does alcohol induce the body to burn more calories?

Les Boissons
— prix nets —

APÉRITIF	25
PASTIS	25
MARTINI GIN	45
AMERICANO	45
GIN-TONIC	55
GIN-FIZ	55
PORTO	25
WHISKY	45

In the October 1997 issue of *Eating Well* magazine, Professor Eric Rimm of Harvard's School of Public Health was quoted as saying, "People who consume moderate amounts of alcohol cut their risk of heart disease by 30 to 40 percent compared to people who abstain." Can you name a drug that could make such a claim? The same article states the evidence now shows that moderate drinking lowers the risk of osteoporosis, diabetes, protects against winter colds and reduces stress and the risk of depression. Researchers found that moderate drinkers were less likely than nondrinkers to die of stroke, respiratory illness, and even cancer (as long as you aren't deficient in folate--make sure to take a supplement of about 400 mcg a day).

It sounds like researchers are just now catching up with something France has been practicing for a long time. Let me be very careful and remind you that 100,000 people each year die from alcohol-related diseases, ignoring the many more that perish in auto crashes related to drinking. Therefore, you must be very careful to consume no more than what I have suggested--two glasses of wine a day for men--one for women.

Even *Better Homes and Gardens* is now suggesting it's okay to drink in moderation. In their October 1997 issue, they talk about the French Paradox. "In France and other Mediterranean countries, such as Greece and Italy, people dine on plenty of meat, butter and cheese. The paradox is that these people have the lowest rates of death from coronary heart disease in the Western world and suffer only one-third the heart attacks Americans experience. The French prescription for living a healthy, longer life includes rarely eating a meal without a glass or two of wine."

The French Alimentary Groups[5]

It is already confusing enough to try to assign food to a given category since many foods contain components of more than one group. For example, beef contains both fat and protein, beans contain both protein and carbohydrate. Nevertheless, although the French recognize the above groups, they also group foods into a new set of categories, the Alimentary Groups.

CUISINE POUR RESTER MINCE

"Cuisine Pour Rester Mince" Compagnie Internationale du Livre, Paris— an excellent reference for French dieting

THE MINERAL SALTS

The most important of these is table salt, or sodium chloride, contained in all foods in varying amounts. Once thought to be a culprit in hypertension and scrupulously avoided, it is recognized now even here that an adequate amount of salt is required to prevent dehydration, and a hydrated body is very important for health.

Calcium plays an important role in bones and teeth, the coagulation of blood, muscular contraction and cardiac rhythm. The best source is milk. Phosphorus also plays an important part in maintaining the bony skeleton, and is found in milk, eggs, fish and fruits. Magnesium, another important mineral, is found in fruits, grains, and seafood.

TRACE ELEMENTS

Iron, the fundamental element in hemoglobin, is found in meats, certain vegetables, fruits and chocolate. Iodine is found in seafood (and here in iodized salt) and is essential to the thyroid gland. Copper, cobalt and zinc are also important.

VITAMINS

Vitamins are divided into fat-soluble and water soluble groups. The fat-soluble vitamins are essential for night vision and the skin (A and B3), prevention of rickets and absorption of calcium (D), fertility and muscular balance (E), the clotting mechanism (K), and to prevent anemia and spinal tube defects in the newborn(folic acid or B9). Folic acid is also very important in the immune system. These are found in fish oils, milk, egg yolks, vegetables and meat.

Cellulose is indispensable in intestinal transit, and is found in plant matter.

Water is the "source of life".

1. Foods rich in animal protein
These also contain mineral salts and fat, ranging from (very approximately) lowfat examples such as game and rabbit (5%), fish (1-15%), chicken (10%),eggs (12%), duck, some pork and lamb (25%), beef (25-30%), goose (30%), sausage and terrines (30-40% and up).

2. Milk products and its derivatives
These are rich in calcium; milk in particular is a  very complete food. Note that sweetened evaporated milk contains 168 g. of sugar and 700 calories per liter--close to heavy cream! Yogurt is very close to milk in nutrition and is produced by fermentation. Cheese are rich in protein, and the fat content varies tremendously from 0% to 75%. It is necessary to know the fat content of the cheese you are using! Note that in France, all cheeses are marked as to fat content.

3. Fats
The butter used in France in cooking is almost always what we call sweet butter, and that our salted butter is only sweet butter with salt added. We will use sweet butter in all of our recipes that call for butter. Some oils handle heat better than others, therefore should be used only for specific purposes. For example, corn, olive, or sunflower oils cannot be used above 325°F (or they'll burn), peanut oil can withstand higher temperatures (to 375°F), and is commonly used in France for frying. Extra-virgin olive oil is wonderful cold, for example on salads, but loses much of its taste when heated and is therefore wasted on frying.

4. Flours, Grains, Cereals

The cereal grains are composed of an envelope, rich in cellulose, and the grain itself, rich in protein, mineral salts and B1. Whole grain cereals are therefore much more complete and healthy. Sweet doughs, cookies and pastries represent a combination of sugars, fats and flours that are the worst for any diet.

5. Beans
These are very rich in proteins and carbohydrates, calcium, iron, and, unfortunately, calories.

From the author's kitchen, while staying in Juan-les-Pins, Antibes

6. Fruits and Vegetables
There are common features including the presence of carbohydrates, cellulose, lots of water, vitamin C and mineral salts. They are low in lipids and proteins, as well as calories. While they contribute little to the daily calorie intake, they contribute a great deal to nutrition. Potatoes are closer to cereals in starch and calories, like rice and pasta.

7. Sugar
Important to cooking, but also important not to overindulge.

8. Drinks
Water is the source of life, the most abundant constituent of living matter. An adult needs about 40 g. of water per kg. of body weight, per day. Half of this requirement is found in the food we eat, the other half must be taken in by drinking water. Remember, what is the first thing they do to any patient presenting with almost any serious complaint at the Emergency Room? They start an intravenous infusion containing water to hydrate the body. This is because physicians understand that only a properly hydrated body can function efficiently. Take a lesson! All French sources recommend a daily water intake of 1 to 1 1/2 liters per day. You will find bottles of water on every French table at every meal.

It is not necessary, from a nutritional point of view, to balance each meal with adequate amounts of carbohydrate, protein and fat, nor with foods from each of the alimentary groups. The only thing that is needed for a balanced diet is to balance an entire day. If you consume a good deal of carbohydrate, for example at breakfast and lunch, as you will eating dry cereals and salad, then simply include enough protein at dinner--3 to 6 ounces of meat, fish, or poultry. Trying to balance each meal would be a real nightmare!

Mealtime: Le Petit Déjeuner

(BREAKFAST)

The author and breakfast in Lyon

Okay, enough of science! We'll use that information to help us decide how to put a day's meals together that are sufficiently varied in composition to contain all the essential nutrients, but how do we decide how much to eat and how to allocate that to various meals?

The French are notorious for skipping breakfast. Every book I read on nutrition in France has pages devoted to convincing the French to eat breakfast. The excuses are the same as in the U.S., "I am not hungry, I don't have time, Coffee is sufficient, I'm watching my weight....[6]"

Why is it so important to have a small breakfast? The most important reason I can give you is that if you fail to start the day with something, by the time lunch rolls around you will be hungry enough to think that the portion you should eat is not large enough. You will inevitable eat more (in the long run) than both a small breakfast and lunch put together! Eat just enough at breakfast so that you are full--not overfull--and when lunchtime comes you will have no trouble deciding you are full before you overeat.

I know this is heresy to most dietitians who will insist that breakfast should be at least a third of the day's calories, but that severely limits what you can eat the rest of the day. A large breakfast also expands the stomach and for many people, will cause them to be hungrier at lunch time than if they didn't eat it at all. I know that this flies in the face of nutritional convention, but

isn't this a good place for that old saying, 10,000 Frenchmen can't be wrong?

Breakfast at the bar in Paris

Therefore I am recommending a small breakfast, which is a good way to think of a petit déjeuner. No egg omelets (that's lunch or dinner), no fried eggs with ham or bacon or potatoes! The French eat a good deal of fresh fruit and yogurt in the morning, and that's a very good example to follow. If you're not having a fresh fruit with breakfast, a glass of fruit juice should be on the table to drink. As noted before--straight juice--no adulteration with sugar, no "fruit drink". They also eat grains in the morning, for example cereal, both hot and nowadays, more and more cold cereals (we are going to choose whole-grain cereals, without sugar frosting. Prepare these with lait écréme, which is nonfat milk, and artificial sweetener if desired). You may think the tradition of France calls for brioche or croissants, but again the French do not eat every day; rather they are holiday foods.

Try instead a piece of French bread with preserves. This is what I especially like to eat in the

Breakfast No.1		Breakfast No.2		Breakfast No.3	
French bread* 5"x2"x1"	100 cal	cereal 2/3 cup	90 cal	French bread 5"x2"x1"	100 cal
jam, 4 tsp	90 cal	skim milk,4 ounces	40 cal	apple, sliced ***	80 cal
juice**, 4 ounces	50 cal	juice, 4 ounces	50 cal	cheese, 1 ounce ****	100 cal
1% milk, 4 ounces for coffee	60 cal	1%milk, 4 ounces for coffee	60 cal	1% milk, 4 ounces for coffee	60 cal
Total	290 cal		230 cal		330 cal

* Substitute low-fat yogurt here, at times, and use the jam and fruit juice allowance for fruit.
** Substitute fruits of an equivalent calorie count.
*** Substitute 2 pats of butter.
****If you actually like low-cal cheese, use a larger portion for an equivalent calorie count.

Table 1: Three reasonable options for breakfast

morning, especially now that we can get the all natural preserves, either domestic or imported from France, without sugar added. The domestic kind I'm sure you're familiar with, but for a real treat try "St. Dalfour" imported conserves. They are made in the heart of the French countryside by an old recipe from the Loire Valley, and are pure fruit without sugar. They can be ordered by mail from St. Dalfour conserves, 2180 Oakdale Drive, Philadelphia, PA 19125 (now I only wish I got a commission). Avoid slathering the bread with butter!

With breakfast, drink tea, low-cal hot chocolate, or café au lait. Café au lait is often prepared in France in the morning at the local bar. Coffee is made in one of the large capuccino machines, and milk is steamed but not frothed to be added as desired. Both are served separately in stainless steel pitchers, on the traditional zinc bartop.

Café au lait can be prepared at home without the expensive machine. This is the way many French housewives do it at home in the morning (you can be sure they don't own expensive capuccino machines). First, buy a good strong coffee like French roast or an espresso coffee. I admit to liking "Bustelo", which happens to be a Spanish-style coffee but is ground and readily available in many supermarkets and is much less expensive than the French roast from the coffee grinder's shop. Measure it into a saucepan, about a rounded tablespoon per cup, add water. Bring to a boil, turn off the fire, and let it steep about 5 minutes. Meanwhile, heat 1% milk almost to a simmer, but not quite. When the coffee is ready, pour carefully so that the grains remain on the bottom. Add about half a cup of coffee to your cup, then an equal amount of hot milk, and then sweetener if you like it. Both the hot coffee and the hot milk can be placed in stainless steel pitchers on the table, and this is the way you will find it served in most French households in the morning. Coffee in the morning is enjoyed from large cups (larger than our standard coffee cups), unlike later in the day when demitasse cups are used.

Note two things here. One, measurement is crucial. We'll come back to that point. Two, breakfast will occupy a varying percentage of the days total caloric intake, depending upon which breakfast is eaten in any given day, and depending on the total caloric intake projected for that day. In general, aim for about 25% of the days total intake, or less. A 300 calorie breakfast is about 25% of a 1200 calorie diet, so there should be no trouble arranging this, given the choices above.

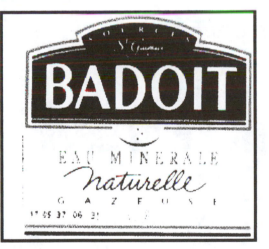

PRINCIPLE NUMBER 11:

Drink six glasses of water per day. Put a bottle of water on the table at every meal. Keep your glass out permanently!

On the table at breakfast should be a bottle or pitcher of water. The water should be refrigerated, but does not require ice. The French drink a good deal of water, and this is one of the secrets to thinness. Adequate hydration is extremely important. One liter, or about 6 of our glasses, is to be consumed daily, starting with breakfast. I, personally, hate the taste of tap water, so I, like most of the French (despite the advice of our French author above) drink bottled water. I drink either Perrier or soda water, and don't find much of a problem with distension from the carbon dioxide. If you do, drink still water. I try not to drink 6 glasses of Perrier, one, because it's expensive, and, two, because of the mineral content. I switch off with refrigerated tap water or soda water. The variety in water is good. However, if you are young, with good kidneys, mineral water probably won't be a problem.

Never take fluid pills thinking you're going to lose weight. Fluid pills are appropriate for those with high blood pressure, or certain heart and lung conditions where there is a fluid buildup. Now I've had any number of 300 pound patients walk into my office, poke a finger into their rotund stomachs, and complain, "you see, I'm just all filled up with water; I need a water pill!" Sorry, but that isn't water, it's fat. The only thing you accomplish with fluid (or "water") pills is dehydrating yourself.

Let's think why that's dangerous. Remember what I said about the first thing that happens in an Emergency Room, almost no matter what is wrong? An intravenous infusion is started to run fluid into your veins and "re-hydrate" you. This is because as physicians we know that dehydration is an enemy of the body's ability to fight off disease or heal. So the last thing you want to do is dehydrate yourself.

Déjeuner

(LUNCH)

Salad Niçoise as eaten in Nice

Traditionally in France, lunch was the big meal, just as it was in rural America years ago. For the same reasons, it is no longer so. People no longer have the luxury of enjoying lunch as a family gathering, as was done then. Women stayed home and prepared a big meal all morning, men returned for a refreshing break from their manual labors, and all sat around the table for a grand repast. Lunch time in France is still apt to be two hours in many places, because the tradition is so entrenched there. However, in cities it is unlikely to be a big meal as working people rush around, trying to fit in their dental appointments, picking up a few things at the store, and barely leave time to swallow a sandwich. Also, more and more women are working in France, and don't have time to prepare a large lunch. Many are trying to advance at their jobs and nibble at a hard egg with a cup of espresso.

The result, as described in "La Meillure Cuisine Minceur" is "a sidestepped lunch, insufficient, often taken in bad conditions (standing, in the corner of the office, or elbow to elbow in a coffee shop), and a generator of stress".

"At noon, even if you have little time to eat, organize a meal for yourself. Dedicate this break fully to eating.

"If you arrange to go to a restaurant for lunch, it is excellent. It is up to you make good choices from among the things that are suggested. If you carry your lunch, prepare it the day before in the evening: varied composed salads, cold meat that may remain from the weekend, hard-boiled eggs or ham, a fruit, a piece of cheese. If a sandwich is sometimes unavoidable, choose sandwiches of ham, of vegetables, or of cheese, rather than of rillettes (a cold paste of diced pork and pork fat

Déjeuner	1200 cal	1500 cal	1800 cal
Crudités*	3.5 ounces	3.5 ounces	3.5 ounces
Oil**	1 teaspoon	1 teaspoon	2 teaspoons
Meat or equivalent***	3.5 ounces	3.5 ounces	4.5 ounces
Green vegetables	5 ounces	5 ounces	5 ounces
Starches		3.5 ounces	3.5 ounces
Bread			1 ounce
Cheese or equivalent		1 ounce	1 ounce
Fresh fruit	5 ounces	5 ounces	5 ounces
Total calories	290	490	590

Anne Noël, French dietitian and author, suggests this for lunch from Maigrir [4]

*Crudités are raw fruits and vegetables
** Oil can be used to make the traditional oil and vinegar dressing, vinaigrette, or better yet, I suggest a calorically equivalent amount of regular or lowfat (not necessarily fat-free) dressing. One teaspoon of oil is about 35-40 calories, and dressings vary, but you can easily find one that will allow 2 table-spoons or more for 40 calories.
***The amount of meat can be adjusted based on its calorie content--more of fish, less of red meat--so that the total comes out right. Don't feel you must use up this allowance at lunch; shift it to dinner if you like.

Table 2: What to do about lunch

cooked in lard), sausages or hot-dogs. Finish the meal with a fruit and a yogurt.

"Lunch should include:
>   -a protein contribution: meat, fish, eggs or ham
>   -a dish of vegetables and/or of the starch family
>   -cheese, milk, custard, fruit fresh or cooked
>   -bread"[6]

The book goes on to detail the evils of too much to eat at dinner. This brings up an interesting point: Is it true that if one eats one's main meal at dinner rather than at noon, one will gain more weight? That is, if one eats a 300 calorie lunch and an 800 calorie dinner, why should one gain more weight than if one eats an 800 calorie lunch and a 300 calorie dinner? We in this country have been told to avoid eating a heavier meal at night because we'll gain more weight. Is it true? The answer is a qualified no.

The calorie totals in table 3 have been determined by me (just to set the record straight) and are not part of Mme. Noël's table. But, look what a sumptuous lunch you can have!

PRINCIPLE NUMBER 12:
It doesn't make any difference when you eat. What matters is what you eat, and how much of it you eat.

It would appear that we gain more weight by eating at night, because of several things. First, we are much more apt to eat less, even for a "big" meal at lunch than dinner, because we are not as hungry at that hour, or because we have to face an afternoon at work and would be uncomfortable if we ate that much. Therefore, the meals may not actually be calorically equivalent even if lunch is intended as the large meal. Second, we are more apt to drink alcohol or eat dessert with the evening meal, further raising the calorie count. Third, the admonition not to eat at night often refers to snacking, and many snack foods do put on weight fast.

On the other hand, and this is where the qualified part of the answer "no" comes in, there is something to the theory that we burn off slightly more calories if we are active while digestion is taking place, rather than asleep. For these purposes, the amount of difference is not very significant. So, if you, like most of the French nowadays, want to eat you larger meal at night, that's fine.

That being said, lunch should still account for about 30-35% of the day's total caloric intake. At a minimum intake of 1200 calories, that means about 360-420 calories, whereas at 1800 calories one could go as high as 630 calories at lunch.

Here's how to do it:

Decide how many calories to "spend" at lunch. Decide what foods appeal to you at lunch and fit within your lifestyle. Browse the recipe file, or make up your own recipe to fit this outline. That's all there is to it!

An example of a lunch to make at home that fits within the 1200 calorie diet might be a lovely composed salad, consisting of 3 1/2 ounces of cubed ham and quartered hard-boiled egg, 3 1/2 ounces of cold blanched carrots and corn, and 5 ounces of lettuce, broccoli florets and blanched string beans, all served with a homemade vinaigrette. Add a sliced pear for dessert. On higher calorie regimens, add beans to the salad, add an ounce of diced cheese, and add bread on the side. See how it works?

Composed salads have very good memories for me. I walked down the promenade in Juan-les-Pins, the beach at Antibes, on the Côte d'Azur in France. It was, perhaps, 88 degrees. A warm breeze blew off the Mediterranean Sea, to my right. I turned in front of a royal blue awning proclaiming, "Ruban Bleu," the name of one of the beachfront restaurants, and proceeded down the stairs. I was shown a table, practically on the sand. White market umbrellas protected me from the sun. The tables were set with placemats, white napkins, stemware and each had a small flower vase with fresh flowers. Ice cold Perrier arrived. I was steps from the blue Mediterranean. I ordered a traditional dish for this area, a composed salad. It was wonderful!

Converting Mme. Anne Noël's table above into what to actually make for lunch, such as I did here, or learning what to choose from amongst the offerings at a restaurant, is what requires the basic background in Dieting 101 I presented above. Whip out that pocket calculator and paperback calorie list. Keep them in the kitchen, in your pocket, or any place handy, and you will be able to create an imaginative lunch and yet be sure you're well within the guidelines. We'll discuss going out to eat later.

An aside: It is my suggestion that you not announce to the world that you are dieting. First, what you are really doing is just changing your eating habits for the better, as part of a lifetime program. Second, you will have to endure remarks from all corners of the globe about what you are and are not eating. You will also have to endure all the self-righteous comments by friends and coworkers about how they manage to stay so "svelte"--look around--they're not! Third, you will not have to report to all who ask, "So how many pounds have you lost so far?" Finally, you will not have to bear the snickering of others when you decide it's time for a "holiday".

Remember about the bottle of water on the table at lunch!

After lunch, linger over an espresso or a cup of coffee before resuming the day's activities. If you're full before you finish the dish, quit! If you eat alone, and you enjoy reading, I encourage it, as I will explain later. However, remember that while you are actually eating, your attention must be on the food, not your book.

Like I told you about the activities of daily living, also make eating as inefficient as possible. Put down the fork after every bite and chew the food. Don't pick up the fork to eat the next bite until you've swallowed the one you're eating. Take at least a full twenty minutes with the dish, longer if you can. If you're in a hurry (don't be), eat less rather than trying to eat quickly. Take the time to actually enjoy the food. More about this later.

Pastis in Provence, at the bar

Tea or Cocktails

No, I haven't lost it...I know this is a book about French eating habits, and I know tea is thought of as an English tradition. However, the French often stop on the way home from work at a café for a glass of *bière*, or a *Pastis* (this first alternative I know you can translate; the second is an anise-flavor liquor that is clear, but turns cloudy instantly when mixed with water, which is how it's usually served. It's extremely popular in the French countryside; pronounce it pass-TEECE). It's important to the overall plan to end the afternoon with some refreshment, so that you won't be starving (or snacking) till dinnertime. A glass of wine would be acceptable now, in place of what you would drink at dinner, but remember the total amount is one to two glasses per day! A light beer would be okay, but remember that the kinds of snacks that go with beer don't go with dieting, and the effects of the beer or wine this early in the may make you forget about your well laid plans for a sensible dinner, and that would be very counterproductive. You could skip tea and go right to an early supper, but then you'll eat dinner too early! People who eat an early dinner are just asking to be tempted by high calorie snack foods later on in the evening, usually with rather disastrous consequences to the day's calorie intake.

So I'm suggesting tea. It is not at all unusual to see the French in the Patisserie in the afternoon with a pot of tea. Of course, tea could just as well be a cup of hot, steaming low-cal chocolate or an espresso. It could be a glass of chilled ice tea with a few mint leaves for color. How about a homemade low-cal Perrier-menthe? Be careful, mint syrup is quite high in calories. You can make a low-cal version with fresh mint or mint flavoring, sugar substitute and Perrier. Go light on that ice, the French don't use much, and besides it would just dilute the taste of the Perrier.

I like a nice hot pot of tea accompanied by a biscotti (if not heavy on the nuts, about 65 to 100 calories). Or perhaps about 17 fat-free potato chips. The ones with Olestra are great-tasting, and amount to 75 calories or so. A half cup of lite cheese crackers only contains about 65 calories. Pretzels might be about the same. We're so fortunate these days that the calorie count is printed on the box on most foods in the U.S., these days. It's no longer Russian roulette! You could also substitute a fresh fruit. Pick carefully, choose something you like. During the afternoon, when you think about a snack, just remember you'll have this to look forward to. I like mine about four or five o'clock, depending on how busy I am, and it holds me until dinner.

Dîner

(DINNER)

We have so far used up between 240 and 340 calories at breakfast, between 290 and 590 calories for lunch, and 75 to 100 calories at tea, for a grand total of about 600 to 1000 calories. 1200 calorie people, you're at the low end of that, and 1800 calorie people are at the high end. For you one the 1200 calorie diet, this leaves about 600 calories for dinner, and for those of you at the higher end about 800. This works out to about 40 to 50% of your calories at dinner. You should know that this also is directly contradictory to most diet plans, which allocate the meals evenly, or suggest you should be eating lightly at dinner.

One reason that this is important is that if your family is like mine, dinner is the one meal we all get to share together. It must be something to look forward to, as I do. It also is harder to remain on a diet when you're eating lettuce leaves at night, while everyone else is cutting into a roast. The French are more and more eating their main meal in the evening. This is supposed to be a way of life, and if it is going to be that, it has to be compatible with the style of life that most of us are living!

Will you lose less if you eat your larger meal at night? We started the discussion of this point with a qualified no. But it might look like you're losing less. Take your "twin" of exactly equal weight and metabolic rate, and assume you're both dieting except your twin is eating the larger meal at lunch. If both of you weigh in the morning, your twin will appear to weigh less. That's simply because 7 or 8 more hours will have passed since the twin's larger meal. You would weigh less if both of you always in the mid-afternoon. The bottom line is, eating at night isn't going to make a significant difference, and if that's what'll keep you on the program, fine.

PRINCIPLE NUMBER 13:

Don't try to balance every meal. It's enough if you balance the whole day in terms of intake.

What this means is that if you only eat a salad for lunch, bank those calories and go ahead and enjoy a richer dinner. But, you must plan it--you can't eat a full lunch and a heavy dinner. Try to balance the entire day. If you have an important luncheon engagement, perhaps you'll choose to use your wine allotment then rather than at dinner. If what you choose is more caloric than your plan allows, make up for it in the other two meals. You might have a light breakfast, and a light dinner that day. The only guiding message here is to be sure to compensate within the day for an excess of calories at any one meal.

Diner	Dinner No. 1	Dinner No. 2	Dinner No. 3
Appetizer or soup	About 100 cal	About 100 cal	About 100 cal
Salad, primarily *green**	5 ounces	5 ounces	5 ounces
Salad dressing	1 tablespoon or 20 calories	1 tablespoon or 20 calories	2 tablespoons or 40 calories
Meat or equivalent	3.5 ounces	3.5 ounces	4.5 ounces
Sauce	1 tablespoon	2 tablespoons	2 tablespoons
Red wine	4 ounces	4 ounces	4 ounces
Green vegetable	5 ounces	5 ounces	5 ounces
Added oil or fat**,total	2/3 tablespoon	2/3 tablespoon	1 tablespoon
Starch			3.5 ounces
Lo-cal frozen yogurt	3 ounces	4 ounces	4 ounces
Total calories	600	670	800

* *Be very careful of what you put in salad. Leafy greens and most vegetables are fine. Just a few sprinkles of bacon bits, hard boiled eggs, or seeds and nuts can double the calorie count of a salad.*

** *This is the fat used in the preparation of any of the dishes.*

Table 3: A basic outline for dinner

The following table, like all the ones before it, is intended as a guide to show you how your calorie selections could be allocated. It is not meant to indicate that you must eat, for example, 3.5 ounces of meat at dinner. Some nights you may eat an eggplant dinner, for example, or pasta. Simply adjust the amounts so that they fall within the calorie guidelines. Yes, you can even save your meat calories from lunch if you're having a heavier meat dinner, and need them then. Remember, its not when you eat, but how much and of what that counts! This is also contrary, I realize, to traditional dietary teaching that insists on balancing every meal.

You'll notice in the table below that I recommend a portion size for meat or its equivalent of 3.5 ounces. This corresponds to a 100 gram serving, which is the standard size of portion one often sees in the French cookbooks aimed at healthier cooking. Even in a restaurant in France, a steak will rarely exceed 6 to 8 ounces. Compare that to the oversized 16 ounce T-bone, falling over the edges of the plate, that you're used to seeing in American restaurants. Who's going to live longer when you get done eating?

It may help--especially when eating out and weighing isn't possible--to remember that a piece of chicken (for example) that weighs 100g or 3 1/2 ounces is about the size of cassette tape. Just picture that sized piece and you'll have a good idea how much to eat.

A few hints about salad dressing before you tell me you can't eat salad with so little dressing. Remember you can substitute a larger amount of a lower-cal dressing, if you like. Do not pour the dressing on the salad in the salad dish. Put your salad in a mixing bowl, add the dressing and toss well. Then put it in you salad dish. You'll find the dressing goes a lot farther because it coats each piece of lettuce much better.

If you're eating out, ask for the dressing on the side. It's easier to control how much you are going to use that way. On days when you're really being careful, try dipping your fork into the dressing on the side, then take a forkful of salad. You'll get the taste of the dressing with each bite, but use less dressing.

You'll notice clearly that dinner does include a glass of red wine, and men can have two! Although I included the wine in the calorie count, as you remember from what I said earlier, it may not be necessary to do so. We are just going to play it as safe as possible.

Dinner is concluded with a cup of espresso, coffee, or tea. If you use milk in your coffee or tea, those calories will need to be figured in, but may not amount to much if the quantity is small. Don't forget to put a bottle of water on the table, and drink from it so you can make up your total of 6 glasses of water for the day.

You'll find that these calorie totals are within 50 calories of the day's goals as set out above. You needn't have every course every night, for example if you were on a 1200 calorie diet and used all the breakfast calories and lunch calories on a certain day, skip the soup at dinner! If you're on an 1800 calorie plan and ate a smaller lunch, add a 100 calorie serving of French bread. Starch (potatoes, rice, pasta) need certainly not be served every night, but I intentionally added it to the larger plan so that none of you he-men can tell me you're going hungry.

Remember the bottle of water on the table (I can't say it enough times), and leave your glass permanently out.

A lovely plate of red mullet as served in Juan-les-Pins--but pay attention to the portion size! This is the right size!

PRINCIPLE NUMBER 14:
Pay close attention to portion size.

If you've eaten at a restaurant in France, you know that the amount of meat or chicken on the plate is much smaller than what we think of as routine for a restaurant plate here in the U.S. I'm not saying that any restaurant portion size is the standard, I'm only using it as an example that the French in general eat smaller portions than we do, and this is something it may take a little while to get used to. But, you'll benefit all the way around in the long run, since we all know that our portion size of meat here in this country is too big, giving us too high an intake of protein and fat, particularly cholesterol. This is one of the reasons that the "food guide pyramid" suggested for good nutrition by the Federal Food and Drug Administration here was recently revised, showing now no more than 10% of daily intake from protein.

Remember when you eat out that the restaurant has got to serve a portion size that's going to satisfy a 6'4" athlete, so naturally if you're only 5'2" and sit in front of a computer all day it's crucial that you learn to eat only *some* of what is served. Be guided by the amounts you prepare at home, based on the tables above. Refer also to the section on the clean plate club, coming up!

A recent article in the *New York Times*, by Marian Burros, will show you the dangers here. An experiment was described in which four health professionals were asked to estimate the fat and calorie content in a plate of risotto. Their estimates ranged from 500 to 1000 calories, and from 25 to 70 grams of fat. An independent lab tested the dish, and it was found to contain 1,280 calories and 110 grams of fat! As you can see, not even the professionals can estimate the size of a portion and its contents well. Let the buyer beware!

Estimating food portions at home is no picnic either: It is vital to measure. Buy a good kitchen scale and use it all the time. If you don't, when you prepare food at home what you will find is that a few of your estimated portion sizes and ingredients may be just a little bit larger than actually intended. Over the course of a day, these little increases in caloric consumption will add up, and at day's end you will have consumed just a few more calories than you thought you had. Of course, you may not realize why, but your weight won't drop. Then you will be saying things like, "I've tried, and it doesn't work." Don't set yourself up for failure. Always measure.

Another reason to have a kitchen scale, preferably an electronic one (no, they're not that expensive nowadays) is that true French recipes measure many ingredients by weight, so most French kitchens have a scale. Recipes have been translated here to American volume measurements in most cases, but I want you to get accustomed to the French way and perhaps even try a few from the original French! Did you know that you can translate recipes from French to English by accessing a translation program for free on the internet? Type the following address into your web browser: *www.babelfish.altavista.digital.com/cgi-bin/translate?* Access recipes from Yahoo France ("recette" or "cuisine"), and you're in business!

A Radical Operation on your Eating Habits

Starting over.

At first, it's best to drop your caloric consumption drastically, to make a change in the routine for your body. Contrary to all nutritionists advice, I recommend a radical operation on your intake. Can you fast for an entire day, with nothing but liquids? If you can, it's a great way to get started. There is such a thing as "shrinking the stomach", a necessary thing to adapt to your new style of eating. It is necessary to accustom yourself to new, smaller portion sizes, and to do so, you will need to have a few days of very low calorie intake. To avoid being hungry later, it's a good idea to try to make it the first day on nothing but liquids.

The next two or three days should be a new beginning (forgive the cliché) in your eating habits. For these few days, your calorie consumption should be in the 800 calorie range. This can be easily accomplished by large fluid intake, accompanied by meals of salads and soups. Check the recipe file for some good ideas. I recommend breakfasting on coffee and fresh fruit, then something like a salad of spinach, romaine, or leaf lettuce, accompanied by onions, red cabbage, carrots, and the like with a diet dressing for lunch. Remember it's only for a few days. Dinner should be a large bowl of vegetable soup, a small salad, and a small dessert such as the low-cal frozen yogurt. This will make for a very small calorie count, and will start you off well.

The point of all this is to "shrink your stomach". You will be very surprised at how large the amount of food you will be eating will seem when coming from the vantage point of having started here, rather than from your regular diet. This should also have a very beneficial affect on your appestat, which will be regulated downward by this maneuver. We're talking only about two to three days, now. Are you up to the challenge?

How to Eat

Starting with the very first day, I am going to recommend changes in your regular pattern that will help you to get the most out of your food. Since you will be eating less, you will need to concentrate on your food more. Whether you are dining alone, or with a whole family, set an attractive table. Table settings are not just for company. And if they were, I can't think of any company more important than you. Start from breakfast.

PRINCIPLE NUMBER 15:

Set a proper table, and eat as inefficiently as you can.

Take the time to set the table. Set out pitchers for things, rather than cartons or cans on the table. At lunch at work, if you bring your own, make it as proper a picnic as you can. It will really help you to enjoy the food. At dinner, lower the lights (research shows you eat less in dimmer light), add candles, set out real napkins, a tablecloth once in a while, wine glasses, and be sure to serve the meal in courses.

Be certain to use utensils to eat, regardless if no one is looking. This is very important--don't eat with your fingers. Think about the amount of food you could eat if you just picked up a whole roast chicken and ate it with your fingers, as opposed to a knife and fork. Strive to make

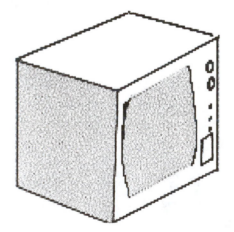

the eating as civilized as possible, because civilized eating is intentionally inefficient, and that's exactly what we want.

Don't make a separate diet meal for you and a "regular" meal for the rest of the family. Simply prepare these recipes for the whole family, and add some bread or potatoes or pasta on the side to fill up those who need more. Be careful that you are not tempted. Dinner time should be a family time, so if you are conversing, follow this simple but extremely important rule.

PRINCIPLE NUMBER 16:
Don't eat while someone is talking to you.

You can't pay adequate attention to your food while listening to someone else. Simply put down your fork until they are finished speaking. Amazingly simple, but it works! One thing that it will accomplish is to prolong the eating experience, and that is very important to our 20 minute rule mentioned previously. Remember you must take at least 20 minutes, longer if you can, to eat that main dish. Remember also to put down your fork between bites, and don't pick it up again until you've swallowed!

Especially if dining alone:
Watching television while eating is often a mistake, but reading is not. Here's why: When you watch television, you cannot arrange the breaks to suit you. Therefore you pay attention to the TV program, and before you know it, the food on your plate is gone! Now be honest, has that never happened to you? On the other hand, you can eat a little, and then read a little to take a short break from eating--it's just like conversing at the table--it helps you to prolong the meal. Just be sure you stop eating when you read, and vice-versa.

Eating out or eating at home...

...the same rules are going to apply. As you read the next few sections, imagine yourself first eating dinner at home either with family or alone, whatever is routine for you. Then imagine yourself eating out. The very same instructions will apply to those restaurant meals, and are even be more important there. I find that I need to get out of the office at lunchtime to change the scenery a little, so I eat at a restaurant almost every day at lunch. Careful selection from a menu at even the most calorie-laden fast food joint will allow you to maintain your eating standards anywhere. More about that later.

Now, several times I've talked about paying attention to the food. What I mean is, as you eat you think to yourself...is this tasty?...is it properly cooked?...would other spices have improved it?...what is the texture of this food?...what other side dishes would complement this dish? Of course, you may think of many more, but be sure you are aware of the food you are eating, or it will slide down and you'll wonder where the food went.

PRINCIPLE NUMBER 17:
The first and second bites of each food item are the most important.

This is true because if you've never noticed it before, those are the ones in which the taste of the food seems most pronounced. There is a scientific reason for this, having to do with taste bud fatigue. Therefore if you concentrate on the taste of the food with the first few bites, and can separate mental hunger from physical hunger you may find that you don't need to finish the entire dish.

PRINCIPLE NUMBER 18:

Mental hunger and physical hunger are different.

When your stomach is growling and you feel rather empty inside, that physical hunger. But if that is not happening, yet you feel like something to eat, that may only be mental hunger. Why it's critical to separate them for yourself is that mental hunger is what's making you overweight, not physical hunger. Our appestat is wrongly adjusted because we've learned to ignore physical hunger and physical satiety and instead eat when we feel mental hunger. If you're concentrating on the first few bites of each dish, and then paying attention as you eat as described above, the next question you should ask yourself as you continue to eat is, "Am I really still hungry?" This question of course refers only to physical hunger. When the answer is no, stop eating!

I was raised by parents, as you may have been, that made it clear I was to be a member of the "clean plate club". I was taught that I must finish everything on my plate. Though well-intentioned, parents who teach this habit to children inadvertently bestow upon them a lifelong habit which leads to overweight and is very difficult to break. You must stop and ask yourself, when you are halfway through each dish if you are *really* still hungry. When the answer is no, during the early days of this plan, remove the dish immediately so that you are not tempted further. With time, you will be able to leave the dish sitting in front of you and will have developed the discipline not to eat any more of it.

When I am out to eat, and have decided I have eaten enough to satisfy physical hunger, I will often stop the waiter and with a smile ask if he will please remove the dish before I accidentally eat any more of it! I usually get a chuckle in return, and the food vanishes before it gets added to me.

Alternatively, if I am eating at a self-service fast-food restaurant, I may order the dish I want, and scrape part of it into the trash bin *before* I even sit down to eat. I still avoid buffets whenever I can. Everyone has his limits!

You may think this is a waste of food. I admit that it is, but I can't control the portion size that the restaurant chooses to put on its plates--only how much of I choose to eat. As to the issue of expense (not getting what you paid for if you discard part of it), the meal costs exactly the same whether or not all of it lands in your stomach!

Mental hunger of the sort we are discussing is really nothing more than a state of mind. When you ask yourself if you are no longer hungry, also ask, "Am I eating this because I'm physically hungry or because it tastes good?" There are times you will want to finish that special dish because it is truly delicious. More often than not you are eating it simply because it's there on your plate.

When the food is sitting on the plate just calling to you to eat it, think: "Which is more important--who is going to win--me or the food?" And that is how you are going to conquer mental hunger. And you will find that it will work, as long as you remember to do just as I have said. Write these questions out for yourself on a notecard, and keep them with you. Refer to them each time this scenario occurs until you feel you no longer need them--until they become a part of you.

PRINCIPLE NUMBER 19:
The psychological satisfaction of having eaten is not related to the amount you ate, but more to the amount of time you spend at the table.

Let me give you an example. Just the other day I was having pangs of guilt at sitting down to a nice dinner because I had eaten out twice that day, although I was still following these rules. At breakfast I had ordered toast, jam, one poached egg, and coffee, and at lunch a vegetable submarine sandwich. I thought back and suddenly realized that I had only eaten one slice of the toast, and only half of the sandwich. It did not even occur to me until I consciously thought about it, that my calorie intake was perfectly okay that day. I psychologically felt perfectly satisfied, even though I had consumed much less food than I had at first thought!

It's not good to be nagged by thoughts during the day that you have missed out on eating. The more time you spend at the table, the more you will later feel, without consciously thinking about, that you have eaten.

PRINCIPLE NUMBER 20:
As you eat, imagine yourself as a person with thin eating habits.

(Please don't get the idea I'm knocking Americans as you read this--just some of our eating habits.) Watch an average overweight American eat at a deli. Large bites, full mouth, that sandwich is consumed as if it were an appetizer. Still hungry because that took no more than five minutes, they look for more to eat, and down slide the fries. Now, watch someone in Paris eat in a bistro. Delicate bites. Chews thoroughly. Next bite doesn't start for a while. Plays with the food. The plate often looks no more than half eaten when they're done.

The lesson to be learned here is that as you eat, and ask yourself the questions above, try to remember that you are a now a person with thin eating habits. I'm not saying that it's easy to overcome a lifetime of eating habits, but I'm saying it can be done, and it starts with knowing what to do. Follow the example set by the Parisian above. Chew the food thoroughly. Put down the fork for a short rest. Talk, read, then pick it up again. Linger over your coffee as you converse or read. You will end up with more satisfaction from your meal.

But I'm dying for a...

Fill in the blank, it's different for each of us. It's a scientific fact that women crave chocolate more than men do. Of course, all generalizations like that have loads of exceptions, but I find that surprising though it may be, it's true. Conversely, men crave meat more than women do. Women often prefer sweet snacks, men prefer salty. What are you going to do when the craving for that special something hits?

PRINCIPLE NUMBER 21:
When the craving for that special something hits, give in to it. But only eat a little.

Remember that this is a way of life, not a crash diet. If you've just got to have that Snickers bar, or whatever, do it. But, may be you don't need to eat the whole bar. Can you discard half before

Messieur le boucher (the butcher)in Aix-en Provence

you start so that it's not there to tempt you?
PRINCIPLE NUMBER 22:

Don't set unrealistic weight goals for yourself.

Remember you are not on a crash diet, this is a way of life! Set a goal of losing 10% of your current weight. Even that amount will improve your looks, have you feeling better about yourself, and reduce your health risks. After you've lost the 10%, go on an intentional holiday but watch closely that you eat just enough more to maintain the loss without actually gaining weight. Try to hold your weight there for a few months, and you will find it very easy at that point to get a little stricter and lose another 10%. Remember the tortoise won the race! Lose weight slowly but consistently over time, and it will stay off.

Dying for a steak-frites? Many of the wonderful bistros in France serve a grilled steak with fries. Did you know that some of those steaks are horsemeat? If you didn't, and you can't stomach the idea of horsemeat, don't worry. I can't either. I'm not about to tell you to run to the nearest stable, butcher knife in hand. But it is germane to our point here that beef is not the only steak around. Consider buffalo, which is very lean and much lower in calories. If I sat you down (I actually did this with a friend of mine) and fed you a grilled buffalo strip or rib steak, you might not be able to tell it from fine, aged beef!

Here is a good suggestion for your next birthday or a great Christmas gift to yourself (hint: they're expensive). You can buy New York style strip steaks of buffalo (bison) from many mail-order vendors around the country. They come flash frozen and vacuum sealed, packed in a Styrofoam chest with dry ice or gelpacks. They are sent by overnight air express anywhere in the country. They are DELICIOUS! An 8 ounce steak (your lunch and dinner allowance) is only 248 calories, and taste very much like prime aged beef except without the fat. Can they be any good without the fatty taste? You bet they can! Try them with faux-frites (French-fry cut potatoes seasoned with salt, pepper, and a little olive oil and baked in the oven).

While I'm on the subject of mail-order, many of those same places can supply wild game, pheasant, goose, poussin, rabbit and other delicacies that may not be locally available. These are certainly a special treat and are authentic in a number of good French recipes. While there are many sources, a few that I know sell buffalo are:

Denver Buffalo Company 1.800.289.2833
Game Sales International 1.800.729.2090
Native Game Company 1.800.952.6321

Also, check out the meat counter at you local supermarket. They may now be carrying a brand of beef such as *Maverick RanchNatural Lite®*, which is substantially lower in fat and calories than standard beef. Shop comparatively for price before you order! Buffalo for example, is a rare treat, and is expensive. Also, check out your supermarket's frozen poultry case for rabbit. Rabbit is very popular in France, and is a very mild tasting meat with fewer calories than chicken! If you've never tried it, now's the time.

Weighing In

When and how often should you weigh? The when part is easier, so let's talk about that first. The best time to weigh is first thing in the morning, without clothing. That way there's no variation for the weight of the clothing you have on. There are also no excuses like, "I must be wearing very heavy shoes since my weight appears to be up." How often to weigh is harder to answer, for this reason. Most nutrition experts will tell you to weigh only once a week because there are fluid shifts in the body (which are very normal) that are going to make your weight go up or down. These fluid shifts will occur regardless of your eating habits those particular days, and so your weight doesn't appear to be responding to dieting at those times...frustrating!

Many people are psychologically so dismayed to find out three weeks into dieting for example,

that for several days or a week running their weight is not down (or even is up), that they go off the diet. Be forewarned that sometimes your weight is controlled by these fluid shifts in your body and has nothing to do with your eating habits. An obvious example for a woman might be the fluid retention that occurs normally before her period, causing a temporary weight gain. This is normal, don't try to fix it. Men also have hormonal and fluid shifts, though it's not as easy to explain why.

Your weight will drop to where it's supposed to be in a few days, as long as you keep to the plan. If you're the type who is fragile about that kind of thing and think you might chuck in the towel, don't weigh but once a week. If you think you can handle it and won't quit out of disappointment, you can weigh daily but expect shifts.

Another point that has to be made here is that a person's weight does not decline according to a nice, gradual slope, no matter how carefully they eat. First, when you start to diet, you lose fluid that is being held in the liver and in fat cells, so your weight drops fairly rapidly. Then you go into a plateau phase when your weight appears to stabilize regardless of how little you eat. This is because the body is now beginning to lose actual fat, and fat breakdown at 3500 calories per pound takes time. If you keep to the plan, all of a sudden one day your weight will appear to drop again, and then stabilize again, following a zigzag downhill course. This is normal. Occasionally, you may discover that your weight is up slightly. Once again, ignore it, keep to the plan, and it will go back down.

The Fast-Food Interlude

"Okay, I'll stick with it, but I eat out at fast-food joints for lunch. What should I eat there?" Interesting that more and more of the French are finding themselves doing that as well, these days. Fast food is part of our way of life when you live in America; even the nutrition experts end up there when time is short.

Here's what to do about it:

Arby's serves three light sandwiches that combined with a small salad weigh in at less than 350 calories. These include Light Roast Chicken Deluxe (276 calories for the sandwich), Light Roast Turkey Deluxe (260 calories), and Light Roast Beef (324 calories).

Burger King has a grilled chicken salad that without the dressing is 200 calories, and light dressing is available. A garden salad is 115 calories with 2 tablespoons of low-cal Italian dressing. Be careful: BK's broiler chicken sandwich is 550 calories! A regular hamburger is 330 calories.

Chick-Fil-A offers a char-grilled chicken sandwich at 258 calories, and a Lite char-grilled chicken deluxe at 266 calories. An 8-pack of nuggets is 287 calories.

Hardee's Grilled Chicken Salad is 280 calories, the Regular Roast Beef is 270, and the Grilled Chicken Sandwich is 290 calories. The regular hamburger is 270 calories.

Kentucky Fried Chicken's Tender Roast breast without skin is 169 calories, and the thigh is 106 calories.

McDonald's has a regular hamburger at 260 calories. Chicken McNuggets (where available) are 290 calories without the sauce.

Subway's Veggie and Cheese Sub is a nice change. Ask for the wheat bun--it's tastier and healthier. Total: 258 calories. The Turkey Sub is also a reasonable choice, and weighs in at 312 calories.

Wendy's plain baked potato is 250-300 calories depending on size, and with cheese topping that comes to 590 calories so stay away! But, there's a great salad bar so Wendy's is no problem. A small hamburger is 260 calories, and an 8 ounce portion of chili is 260 calories.

White Castle's hamburger is 160 calories, but don't eat 'em by the sackful!

Those Fat-Free Magazines

Every magazine with fat-free this and that must arrive at my house. While I enjoy reading them, and have certainly enjoyed some of their recipes, I find too high a percentage that simply don't work. I sometimes wonder if anyone at the magazine has actually tried to make the recipe before it's printed. I also find myself inundated with too many recipes in any one issue to get serious about them. I read them, promise I'm going to have to try them, and file them away.

We're not going to do that here. I'm not going to flood you with choices precisely because I don't want that to happen. I would rather have you get accustomed to the good recipes here one at a time. Plan ahead. Take time when you have it, such as on a weekend, and make several new recipes. Some of them will freeze, others will keep in the refrigerator a day or two for use during your busier midweek. Choose those you like and make them again in a rotation. It always goes easier the second time around, when you know what to expect. As more recipe translations become available, I promise to let you know.

Now, start all over...

...and make this philosophy *yours*! In order for you to make a success of this diet, you're going to have to remember the vital points I've made while preparing dinner in the kitchen, while eating out, and everywhere you prepare or eat food. They need to become a part of *you*, like they are a part of me. I therefore suggest that you take pen and paper, go back through this report, and write an outline of notes for yourself to help you remember the most important points. It makes great reading at lunch!

FOOTNOTES

1 "Obesity in Women", APGO Educational Series on Women's Health Issues.

2 Kirschner MA, Schneider G, Ertel NH, and Gorman J. An 8-year experience with a very-low-calorie formula diet for control of major obesity. Int J Obesity 1988; 12:69-80.

3 Antonello,J. How to become naturally thin by eating more. Heartland Book Co., 1989.

4 Maigrir, des Conseils, des Recettes, by Anne Noël, Editions S.A.E.P., Colmar, France

5 Cuisine Pour Rester Mince, Compagnie Internationale du Livre, Paris)

6 La Meillure Cuisine Minceur, Bernard, Drischel, Noël, Simeon de Robert, Truchelut, and Wenzler, published by Opeasi, Lucerne, Switzerland.

Lyon at night. Is it the gastronomic capital of France?

Secrets of
The French Diet
Cookbook
Part 2

CUISINE FRANÇAISE POUR RESTER MINCE
French Cuisine to Lose Weight

Top to bottom: chef's, paring, and boning knives, and a knife steel

Before embarking on the culinary trail that will lead to preparing French dishes simply and easily in your home, and that will be la cuisine *trés Française*, it is necessary to review a few basics about cooking in general. This presents a dilemma, since some of you are already expert cooks, while others of you know only the rudimentary aspects. We will assume a very basic knowledge of cooking, stressing only those things that I think are essential to preparing the kinds of dishes to be found in these pages.

A kitchen must be equipped in a fashion so as to permit you to undertake the preparation of almost any dish listed without the need for trips to the store for new equipment, especially extra, unnecessary gadgets. These would unnecessarily clutter up your cabinets, and yet, a few things are required to permit you to proceed. Search amongst your kitchen tools now, and see if you don't have these things already. If you don't, this is a good time to consider the purchase of a few good basics.

Knives

The first and most basic requirement in any reasonable well equipped kitchen is a set of good knives. When I say a set, I do not mean a matching set of the finest knives available, nor I mean the kind of knives your average supermarket has on display. Supermarket quality knives allow you to prepare a few meals, and then they dull, never to be useful again. A knife must be as sharp as a razor, or it will mash up and tear at your food instead of slicing and cutting it properly. These kinds of cheap knives are, in fact, not only a waste of money because they are so inferior, but they are dangerous as well.

A dull knife is a dangerous knife. I know that that seems contrary, but it is a simple fact. The largest number of injuries with kitchen knives come from the knife slipping, which it is prone to do when dull, resulting in injury. There are two divergent approaches to keeping a knife sharp enough to cut well. One approach is to serrate the blade, which will mean that the knife will cut without requiring resharpening. This is fine for a bread knife, where ragged edges are not crucial, but if you want to mince garlic or dice tomatoes, it won't do. Serrated knives will tear at your food, making proper cuts impossible. The other approach is to produce a knife with a good blade that will hold an edge for a reasonable period of time. The knife should be of carbon steel or stainless steel, so that it may hold an edge. Carbon steel knives sharpen up to finer edge than stainless, but they do tarnish, pit, and spot badly. More importantly, although their edge is sharper initially, it is not held for as long and requires frequent resharpening. They rust if not

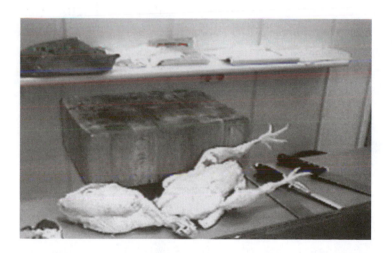

dried well after each use. I therefore recommend stainless steel for general purposes in the kitchen, but if you are willing to care for a carbon steel knife, it is a fine alternative.

A knife steel and three knives are all that are required. You should have a chef's knife, a boning knife, and a paring knife. The first, the chef's knife, should be about 8" long, and have a very wide blade. This blade is made wide so that you can chop or slice with the flat of the blade against your knuckles, to guide the knife without risk. If the blade is not wide enough, you risk slicing at your fingers instead of the food. The blade should be of forged steel, not stamped steel. Cheap knives are generally stamped out of sheet metal, and will not hold an edge for long. A knife should also be balanced when you hold it between your two fingers at the junction of the blade and handle. This saves tremendous effort each time you use the knife to cut. It should also have enough heft to cut through tough food items without having to be forced through. A heavier knife actually make your work easier. Look for a blade that continues uninterrupted all the way through the handle, with three rivets to hold it permanently in place. An exception is the "Global" knife, which is forged in a single piece with a welded hollow stainless steel handle. It has an exceptionally thin and sharp high-carbon stainless blade, and is an excellent choice, from Japan.

The steel is for honing (not sharpening) a knife. To clarify, sharpening is recreating the sharp angle at the blade that makes the knife cut. Honing is straightening out all the microscopic burrs that occur from use, on the very edge of the knife. Honing the knife with the steel should be the first thing you do each time you pick up the knife. Run the length of the knife blade across the length of the steel at about a 20 degree angle first in front of the steel and then in back of it, alternately, about 10 times, and then wipe the blade on the kitchen towel hung on your apron string.

The proper use of the chef's knife is as follows: you hold the heel end of the blade between the thumb and forefinger of your dominant hand, and curl your fingers around the handle. You hold the food item to be cut with the second, third, and fourth fingertips of your non-dominant hand, advancing the joints of the fingers of that hand ahead of the fingertips. You place the flat of the blade against the joints of your fingers, and slice down. Using the thumb and fifth finger of your non-dominant hand, you slide the food item forward toward the knife for the next cut. It takes a little practice, and may feel awkward at first, but is worth learning to do properly. Once learned, it is a lifelong habit that will result in facility with the knife, and safety!

The next knife is the boning knife. This is used for boning and skinning all kinds of poultry, meat and fish, and is important because you may want to buy whole cuts of food rather than pre-trimmed cuts. First, you save money because they are less expensive. Second, you have the bones available for stock, which we'll address shortly. The technique of boning any food item is simple...you want the bones in one pile and the meat in another. Most food have natural cleavage planes to permit this to occur without a great deal of difficulty.

Heavy gauge stainless steel saucepans--these for example are Bourgeat

For example, if you buy a whole chicken, for many recipes you will want boneless, skinless chicken parts. Make a cut between the drumstick and the body of the bird, twist out the drumstick so that the joint between the thigh and backbone is apparent, and cut through the joint. Repeat on the opposite side. Do the same maneuver with the wings to remove them. Make cut down the center of the breast, down to the bone. Pulling the breast meat sideways with your non-dominant hand, slide the knife between the ribs and the meat and continue down to the end of the ribs. Now you have two boneless breasts and two legs. Pull the skin up off one edge of a breast, and slide the knife between the meat and skin right where you see them trying to separate from each other, pulling all the while. There is a natural cleavage plane here that will permit the skin to come off easily, giving you a boneless, skinless breast. Take the remaining carcass and put it in a plastic bag in the freezer. Next time you want to make chicken stock, there you will have one more chicken carcass with which to start. I should point out that all birds are constructed essentially alike, therefore you use the same technique for a duck. This would give you, for example, two nice duck breasts for *Magret de Canard* and two legs for *Cassoulet*. Save the liver for *Œufs à la Bourguinnone* (see recipes). No gourmet butcher is required--just the frozen duck from your local supermarket (surely one of them will carry frozen ducks).

The paring knife is equally essential. It is used for all small functions, such as mincing garlic, creating garnishes, peeling an orange, etc. To mince garlic, proceed as follows: Cut off a snip of both ends of the garlic clove. Roll the clove vigorously between your palms, and the skin will come off easily. Flatten the clove with the blade of the knife. Holding the clove with the fingertips of your non-dominant hand, cut many little slices across the width of the clove, almost to but not through the other side. Now make two cuts through the clove parallel to the table surface, then holding the blade against your knuckles like a chef's knife, slice the length of the garlic in millimeter wide slices. This results in perfectly minced garlic.

Non-stick fry pans--one 8", one 11"

While I hesitate to recommend a particular company's knife, since many are good, a few of the better brands are Wüsthof (German), Global (Japanese), Lamson (American), and Sabatier (French). If there is no good quality kitchen store near your home, these can be bought mail-order, as can the pots I discuss below through catalogues such as: Williams-Sonoma (1-800-541-2233), Sur La Table (1-800-243-6852), A Chef's Catalog (1-800-338-3232), Betty Crocker (1-800-432-4959), Bridge Kitchenware (1-800-274-3435) and Professional Cutlery Direct (1-800-859-6994). There is also a discount outfit called K Sabatier that sells a good French knife at discount at 1-800-526-6399. Comparison shop for price before you decide. Plan on occasional sharpening at your local hardware store, or buy a proper sharpener (stone or electric--Mr. Chef makes a good electric alternative) and learn to use it. Keep your knives in a knife block or on a magnetic holder on the wall. Never throw them in the drawer, or you will dent and chip the blade.

Pots and Pans

The next essential in the armamentarium is a small collection of pots. Not every pot in the kitchen need be of terrific quality, but a few should be good. There is no magic in having a matched set of pots, and I'd rather buy pots matched to the job I want them to do rather than worry about whether or not they match each other (who's looking?). Therefore, my recommendations are different, for each different kind of pot.

There are a few things to look for in a well made pot. Buy a pot with handles that can go in the oven, and preferably handles that stay cool during use. It should be of heavy gauge construction, or it is not going to spread the heat evenly. It should be of a conductive material, or have one sandwiched in its layers, so that it can spread the heat evenly, no matter what size pot it is and what size burner you are using. For an aluminum or copper core to work, it must be at least 1/8" thick--just a copper plated bottom won't do the trick. Cast (not stamped) aluminum is a reasonable choice for a pot, but be aware that aluminum reacts chemically with some foods such as tomato, egg whites, citrus fruits and wine.

A better if slightly more expensive choice is anodized cast aluminum (the charcoal-colored stuff), and better yet is stainless steel with a copper or aluminum core. A copper pot is the best, but to buy a pot of proper weight in copper is quite expensive and requires maintenance for the exterior to look well. A thin copper pot is worse than a good aluminum or stainless one. If you choose a heavy gauge copper pot, opt for a stainless interior rather than the traditional tin, or you will find yourself with a maintenance headache. Tin linings require regular re-tinning, and shops that perform that service are getting harder to find.

I think nowadays, especially with these recipes where we are trying to keep the calorie count under control, it is important to buy fry pans/sauté pans (for our purposes they can be almost interchangeable, but sauté pans really have straight sides) with non-stick interiors. This is not so crucial with saucepans, stock pots, or soup kettles, since fat is not necessary for poaching, simmering and boiling. I have tried one brand of cast anodized aluminum non-stick pan that claims its non-stick is permanent, and permits metal utensils--but it wasn't very non-stick. I have tried another that permits metal utensils and was non-stick, but all the food gets branded with the little design of the non-stick coating. The standard non-stick coatings do not stand up to use with metal utensils, and very few of us can manage to do without them for every dish. Therefore, for fry pans I recommend a cast aluminum pan which is not very costly, such as the kind you can find at your local restaurant supply store. Yes, most of them will gladly sell to the public. Look for Vollrath, Lincoln, or comparable brands. If and when the coating wears, you won't feel heartbroken about buying another. Plan to buy two-- one about eight inches in interior diameter, the other about eleven inches.

On the other hand, for your saucepans, which do not require a non-stick interior, buy the best you can afford and plan to keep them. Any of the mail-order catalogs above have a good selection, and I urge you to compare their features and price. Consider, amongst the many other fine alternatives Calphalon, Tramontina, Look, Berndes, All-Clad, Bourgeat, Sitram, or Chaudier. I recommend you start with a one and a two-quart saucepan as essential, and add other pans as you need them.

A covered casserole or soup kettle is the next and last recommendation. Any of the above manufacturers make excellent examples which are flameproof and can be used on top of the stove as well as in the oven-- a must. Get one that is in the 4 1/2 to 5 1/2 quart range to start. I also recommend the French line of porcelain covered cast iron kettles called Le Creuset. These are excellent and are available by telephone order at discount from a Le Creuset outlet, such as the one at 1-803-589-6650.

Incidentally, a double-boiler is occasionally nice, but not necessary. Just put the food in a stainless steel mixing bowl on top of a saucepan in which water is boiling. This is one of several reasons I prefer stainless mixing bowls. I also like that they don't break, and require less storage room.

So there you have it--three knives, four pans and one pot (the difference is that pans have one single long handle, and pots have two short handles). The balance of pots and pans you need for cooking on a regular basis can be made up of less ideal examples, which you probably already own.

Small Equipment

In the category of other essential equipment, I strongly recommend a kitchen scale, preferably electronic. This is essential here because you must weight some foods accurately or you will not adhere to the portion sizes intended, and may skew the calorie counts substantially. A spring scale will do, but is often considerably less accurate, and tends to become less accurate still with frequent use.

You will need an assortment of measuring cups--any kind will do--and of measuring spoons. The way all dry ingredients are measured here is by the dip and sweep method. You dip up more than the cup or spoon will hold, and sweep across its top with the back of a knife. You won't get as accurate an amount by any other technique.

You will also need a fine sieve, at least four or five inches across, a couple of rubber spatulas, a whisk, a vegetable peeler, melon baller, wooden spoons, a ladle, a spatula, a rolling pin, a cutting board (never cut with those knives on anything else!), a meat thermometer, those mixing bowls, a roasting pan, a few molds, a few ramekins (straight-sided French custard cups), a cookie sheet, some parchment paper, some cheesecloth, and a blender or food processor. Try to get an 8" tart pan that is non-stick with a removable bottom, or an 8" pastry ring. You can put a sheet of parchment paper on your cookie sheet, put the ring on top, and fill it with rolled-out dough. You bake it that way, then slide out the tart shell. I'm sure to have left something out, but really for a complete but basic kitchen these make a good start.

And...

Oh, you'll need a refrigerator, freezer, and a stove--have I left those out? About stoves--some of you have gas and some electric, and they are different. They require different techniques to cook successfully on the, and this is rarely explained. A gas stove heats very quickly and, when you turn down the flame, the heat source is diminished and the pot cools down quickly. An electric burner heats more slowly, and, when turned down, takes a much longer time to cool. Therefore, when using an electric stove with a recipe that requires you to substantially change the amount of heat the pot receives in a short period of time, pre-heat two burners to two different temperatures--for example high and low--and to simply *move the pot* from one to the other. Otherwise it may take too long for the burner to cool down, and the food may scorch. Conversely, move the pot to the pre-heated burner on high when you need more heat, and you won't be waiting for the burner to warm up.

While a gas stove has the advantage of rapid response, it has the disadvantage that it may not be able to keep a pot at a low enough temperature without blowing out. Gas stoves frequently have difficulty maintaining a low simmer, for example. For this reason, a heat diffuser is a good idea. It is an inexpensive metal plate with an air space inside, that goes on top of the burner under your pot, restricting the amount of heat the pot gets.

Kitchen Machines

You could have an unlimited number of them it seems nowadays. There are one or two that are found in more recent times in the French kitchen, and these are worth mentioning. A food processor is a real worksaver, permitting you to make things like mousses with tremendous ease nowadays. A mousse used to require hand chopping of the ingredients and pressing them through a drum sieve, a very tedious process. It is now a matter of a few seconds in the machine. The other machine worthy of mention is an electric mixer, either a stand model or a hand held one. It makes an easy chore of things like beating egg whites, and some can even mix dough. I suggest looking into a heavy duty one for the most wide range of uses.

Ingredients

Three important points to be made here. One, all dry ingredients are to be measured by the dip and sweep method. As noted above, no tamping, patting, or any other method will give you as accurate a measure.

Secondly, more importantly, *all the ingredients for any given recipe should be measured out before you start*. *Read the entire recipe through*, then measure out the correct amounts of what you need. If ingredients need advance preparation--for example dicing or mincing--do it now and then put the results into a ramekin, a custard cup, a paper cup (whatever you prefer).   Collect all the measured ingredients in their containers into one space or even better, place them on a tray. This collection of ingredients, properly measured and prepared, is called your *mise en place* (pronounced *meez en plahs*), and I think is one of the most important distinctions in technique between someone who is serious about their cooking, and someone who is not. It will save countless errors later on, and is an important habit to acquire.

Thirdly, all fresh ingredients should be not only fresh, but *superb* examples of their kind. If excellent produce, for example, is not available at the local store, consider a drive to purchase better quality, then freeze some. If high quality meat is not available, it can be bought out of town and brought back on ice to be frozen, or it can be ordered mail-order. If something is not top-quality because it is out of season, consider using a substitute ingredient--a good example is the use of canned tomatoes instead of fresh in winter (because the taste may be missing in what the supermarket calls "fresh"). A number of my recipes call for canned, dried, or frozen ingredients. Of course, you can always substitute an appropriate amount of fresh ingredients—and you should, if they are available. My point is to show you where you can use frozen or canned ingredients with a very acceptable result, especially if fresh ingredients are hard to find or out of season.

Fourth, all butter used in my recipes is to be sweet butter, not salted. This is traditional in French cooking, and you'll want exact control over the amount of salt you add to a recipe. If you use canned chicken broth instead of making your own, always buy the low-salt variety. Even this has more salt than is ideal, and doesn't reduce well without getting your recipe saltier--so check before you add any salt.

Several recipes will call for a *beurre manié* (pronounced *burr man-YAY*) . This is simply butter and flour kneaded together. Since it is really hard to knead together one tablespoon, or worse, one teaspoon, of each, make up more than you need, and freeze it if you like till you need it again. It's a great thickener for sauces--just be sure you cook the sauce for a few minutes after you add it to get rid of the floury taste.

Some recipes call for a *bouquet garni* (pronounced *boo-KAY gar-NEE)*. This is a bunch of herbs tied in a little roll, usually consisting of parsley, thyme and a bay leaf. Dry herbs can be used, but fresh are preferred. The exact proportions are a matter of taste. Sometimes they a rolled in a small piece of leek and tied up, other times they can simply be tied together with kitchen string--again a matter of preference. In France, for the convenience of home cooks, this collection of herbs can be purchased in a "tea bag" ready to use. The reason that they are tied up is so that they can be removed easily at the end of the cooking process.

One further word about ingredients--the ones we leave out! *In my recipes I often do not list water, salt, pepper, or pan spray.* I make the assumption that these are always immediately at hand and do not have to be listed.

Well, with that in mind we now go to the list of recipes. You will notice that there are relatively these two meals are quite simple unless they are taking their dinner at midday. Also, amongst those of us who work, there is relatively little opportunity or need for extensive breakfast and lunch recipes. However, at dinner time, we have the opportunity to create a little something special—some days a simple French meal— other days a more elaborate one. Therefore, the majority of our recipes are for main courses, leaving you to fill in the gaps with basic fresh vegetables, simply prepared. While it has been much more difficult and time consuming to write a recipe book mostly of main dishes, I think you will find it much more valuable than if I had filled up the pages with intricate or time consuming side dishes that are too much effort to prepare when there's also a main dish to fix—or with breakfasts that would make you get up at 4 AM to start. I am particularly excited about the many recipes from our top-drawer French chefs, without whose inspiration this book book would not have been possible.

Secrets of
The French Diet
Cookbook
Part 3

Basic Preparations

Remember when serving any of these dishes that the visual presentation is extremely important. Remember to set the table properly, using cloth napkins, candles, and tablecloths when appropriate. Set out the water glasses and the wine glasses above and to the right of the base plate. Arrange the silverware carefully, forks on the left, spoons and knives on the right. The French often place the forks tines down (dinner and salad, in whatever order you're going to serve them), and the knife blade faces left. You don't need a teaspoon at dinner. Bring it later when you serve coffee. You may however want a tablespoon for sauce, and if so, place it to the right of the knife (the French often place it bowl down to match the forks).

Remember how important visual presentation is when you arrange the food on the plate. Think ahead when you're planning your meal so that garnishes are at hand when serving time comes. Decide about color balance on the plate so that you don't end up without contrast. Don't forget to preheat the plates. Imagine the finished dish in your head so that you know beforehand how to arrange it. You must decide, for example, whether the fish will look best at the bottom of the plate directly in front of the diner, with the vegetables at the top. Or should you put just the fish on the plate, and surround it with sauce and garnish, putting the vegetables on a side plate. Or do you want the fish sitting on top of the vegetables (as could be done, say, with steamed spinach) in the center of the plate with the sauce pooled in the front?

Neatness counts, too. Wipe all spills before you serve.

Calorie Comparisons

I thought that providing a reference to compare the relative calorie counts of some of the choices you have in cooking might be enlightening. This information can be used to your advantage, for example, when preparing one of the cream sauces such as Velouté. Depending on your own particular calorie requirements, you might choose 1% milk, as listed in the recipe, or you might be able to use fat free half-and-half, for improved taste at a slight caloric cost. At least this way you're choosing from a knowledgeable position. I did the calorie counts myself, using Margo Feiden's The Calorie Factor and *Mastercook* software by Sierra. I think they're as accurate as they can be, given that foods vary.

MILKS AND CREAMS

DAIRY PRODUCTS	CALORIES PER CUP
Cream Cheese	840
Heavy cream	800
Whipping cream	720
Sour cream	480
Neufchatel "Cream" Cheese	480
Ricotta	440
Sour "half & half"	360
Half and Half	320
Evaporated Milk	302
Evaporated Skim Milk	198
Fat Free Half and Half	160
Whole Milk	150
Lowfat yogurt	140
Fat Free yogurt	120
2% Reduced Fat Milk	120
1% Low Fat Milk	102
Buttermilk	99
Skim Milk	86

THE MAYONNAISES

These are the relative values. It's up to you to decide where to draw the line in taste versus calorie count.

Mayonnaise	100 calories per tablespoon
Mayonnaise, light	50 calories per tablespoon
Mayonnaise, lowfat	25 calories per tablespoon
Mayonnaise, fat-free	10 calories per tablespoon

I use the "lowfat" for most things as a compromise between calorie count and taste.

Court Bouillon (for fish)
POACHING LIQUID FOR FISH

A court bouillon is used for poaching many kinds of fish. Variations of the court bouillon are possible. Some recipes call for a quantity of fish trimmings (about 1 pound of trimmings per quart of bouillon), or fish stock (about 2:1), or red wine instead of white with the addition of another chopped carrot. Occasionally champagne might be substituted for the wine, or a few cloves added. Unlike other stocks, the vegetables are sometimes served along with the fish, so peel the carrots if you are going to use them.

3/4	cup	celery, finely chopped
1/2	cup	carrots, finely chopped
1/2	cup	onion, finely chopped
2	tablespoons	butter
1	cup	white wine -- or 1/4 cup vinegar
1	teaspoon	thyme
1		bay leaf
1/4	cup	parsley stalks, chopped
2	teaspoons	peppercorns

Sauté celery, carrots, and onion in butter in a 4 quart saucepan until vegetables are softened. Do not brown. Add wine and herbs, and 3 quarts of water. Bring to a boil, then lower the heat and simmer 30 minutes. Add peppercorns 10 minutes before cooking time is up, then strain (if peppercorns remain in too long, their taste becomes overpowering), placing a cheesecloth or wet paper towel in the strainer.

Now, go to the fishmonger and buy a nice, meaty, filet of fish such as cod or grouper, trim it, poach it just until cooked through (not flaky--that's overcooked and dry), and choose a sauce from the sauce section such as Bercy. There you are, Grouper Bercy...nothin' to it!

CRÊPES

Serves 8

1	cup	flour
3		eggs
1	cup	milk -- (not lowfat)
3	ounces	water
1	tablespoon	butter -- melted
1/2	teaspoon	salt

pan spray or melted butter for pan

Pour all ingredients into bowl of food processor or blender and blend thoroughly for several seconds. Either use immediately or refrigerate and re-blend at time of use.

In France, we tried a crepe maker, but a pan will do as well.

Preheat a 7- to 8- inch non-stick crêpe pan or heavy non-stick fry pan over medium heat. Spray with pan spray or brush with melted butter. Use a 1/8 cup measure as a guide, dipping it into the batter and pouring it quickly on the hot pan. Tilt the pan quickly to spread the batter all over. Cook until small bubbles form on top, which if pan heat is correct should take one minute or less. Insert a metal spatula or icing knife to release edges, and flip crêpe, if you wish to cook the other side. If your crêpes are thin enough, you may not need to. Remove finished crêpe, and stack between waxed paper to hold.

Makes about 18 crêpes, but expect to lose a few, especially until you get the heat of the pan right. May be refrigerated 3 days or frozen one to two months.

99 calories for two crêpes per serving.

See Fruit Tart recipe for one example of a breakfast or lunch idea that is extremely low in calories. See Crêpes Suzette, or Crêpes aux Framboises for a lavish dessert.

Fonds Blanc de Vollaille

CHICKEN STOCK

1		chicken carcass
1	large	onion -- chopped
1		carrot -- chopped
1	rib	celery -- chopped
1/2		bay leaf
2	sprigs	flat parsley -- chopped
1	sprig	thyme -- or 1/8 tsp dried

Coarsely chop up the chicken carcass, and put everything into a soup kettle. Add enough water just to cover, bring to the boiling point, reduce the heat and let simmer slowly ("a lazy bubble") partially covered for an hour and a half, or more, skimming to remove any impurities that float to the top, as needed. Remove any fat on the surface. Strain, and reduce if necessary until you have a flavorful stock. As an alternative, you can use low-salt canned chicken stock instead of some or all of the water, which will give you a richer stock that doesn't need reduction.

You can prepare multiples of this recipe anytime, depending on how much chicken you have, and freeze it. I always recommend that you cool the stock quickly by straining it into a mixing bowl just large enough to hold it, and immersing that bowl in a larger one--or a sinkful--of ice and water. Stir occasionally, and when the stock has cooled, measure it into one and two- cup amounts and pour into plastic zipper-type bags. Lay several flat on top of each other in the freezer, until frozen solid, then arrange as you prefer in the freezer. Be sure to label them!

Defrost the appropriate amount anytime you want some chicken stock for a recipe, or to make a nice low-cal appetizer by adding a few spoons of leftover noodles or rice, a little salt, and a pinch of chopped flat-leaf parsley.

About 40 calories per cup.

Fonds Brun
BROWN STOCK

1/4	teaspoon	thyme
1		bay leaf
3	sprigs	parsley
2	tablespoons	oil
3	pounds	beef chuck and bones
1		onion -- chopped
2	ribs	celery -- chopped
1		carrot -- chopped
1/4	cup	red wine

This stock is used for many preparations including the beef ragout in this book. However, I want you to use your imagination when you have stock on hand in the freezer (see chicken stock for freezing directions). For example, throw a few leftover noodles into the hot stock, a little chopped parsley, and you've got a great low-cal appetizer of beef and noodle soup! Save the boiled beef itself and serve it with Sauce Raifort.

Tie the thyme, bay leaf and parsley in a small piece of cheesecloth if you like, and reserve. It's easier to remove them at the end that way. Add the oil to the bottom of your soup kettle or stock pot, set on medium-high heat, and when hot, add the beef cut up into cubes along with the bones. As the beef begins to warm, add the vegetables and periodically give a good stir so that nothing burns on the bottom. You want the meat and vegetables to brown nicely, but any burning at all will give a bitter flavor to the stock and you will be starting over. Remove the meat and vegetables from the pot, and deglaze the pot with the wine (put the pot on high heat, pour in the wine, and stir to dissolve the brown bits on the bottom). Boil about a minute, return the vegetables and meat to the kettle, add the cheesecloth bag with the herbs, and reduce the heat to low, cooking about 15 minutes. Then add a quart of water, bring the heat up until the water is simmering. Skim off the top, and partially cover the pot (leave about a 1" opening to let steam escape). Then reduce the heat to a very slow simmer (no more than a bubble or two at the surface at any one time), and simmer two hours.

Strain the broth and either use a gravy strainer to remove the fat, or just let the broth cool and the fat will come to the top where it can be skimmed off. A small quantity of broth such as this one quart recipe can be cooled in the refrigerator. If you double the recipe be sure to cool it at this point in an ice bath, as the refrigerator won't be able to cool it fast enough and the broth will sit at room temperature too long for safety. After it is cooled, if you're not going to use it right away, portion it out into plastic zip-lock bags, lay them on top of each other, flat, in a pan in your freezer. When frozen, rearrange them to suit you. Be sure to label them.

Fumet de Poisson
FISH STOCK

2	pounds	fish bones*
1		onion -- chopped fine
1	rib	celery -- chopped fine
6	stems	parsley
1		bay leaf
1/4	teaspoon	thyme
2/3	cup	white wine

*Use fresh lean whole fish, fish heads or bones, with or without the trimmings. Frozen fish may be used, and you may save fish bones and trimmings for stock by freezing. Shellfish leftovers are fine, too. Do not use fish which are fatty or have strong flavors such as salmon, bluefish or mackerel. Put everything into a soup kettle or stockpot, add water just to barely cover, and bring to a boil. Lower the heat, skim off the top with a ladle, and simmer uncovered about 30 to 35 minutes. Strain and use, or see directions for freezing under chicken or beef stock.

Œufs Pochés
(HOW TO MAKE)POACHED EGGS

Serves 2

4		bread slices, low-cal -- toasted
4		eggs
1	teaspoon	salt

After toasting the bread, use a biscuit or cookie cutter to cut a circle in the toast as large as each slice will allow, and reserve these rounds. Discard the crusts.

Fill a fry pan half full of water, add the salt, and bring to a boil. Turn down the heat to just below a simmer, so that there is no bubbling action at all. Place each egg in a cup or custard dish, and two at a time, slide them from the cup into the water. After about 3 to 5 minutes, depending on how well-cooked you like your eggs (you want them well-cooked if you live in an area where Salmonella is a problem), use a slotted spoon to remove the eggs to a cutting board. Trim the ragged edges with a knife, then slide them onto the toast rounds, and serve, hot.

To prepare these ahead, remove them one to two minutes earlier, and lower them gently into ice water to stop the cooking. Drain, and store under plastic wrap in the refrigerator until ready to use. Reheat them in barely simmering water for about a minute, and serve.

Note: For some preparations you might like to substitute tartlette shells for the toast rounds.

Serving Ideas : See Œufs Pochés Mornay, for example.

207 calories each (two eggs and two toast rounds each).

Pâte à Tarte
TART CRUST

Making a tart crust low-cal is a real challenge. There is no shortage of low-cal recipes, but few are

workable and fewer still are tasty, unless the calorie count approaches that of a real tart crust. This one is good, but the sacrifice is that there are no real "sides" to the crust. It has a much better taste than the 12 or 15 other ways I tried to make it! The picture shows 4 tries--the winner for taste, hands down, is the one at the back.

Serves 8

1/4 cup sugar
1 egg
1/2 tsp. vanilla   extract
1/4 tsp.almond extract
1/2 cup flour
1/4 tsp. baking powder
1 tablespoon oil

To make eight individual tarts, use tartlette pans no larger than 3 1/2" in diameter. For a single tart, use a tart pan of about 9". For individual tartlets, adjust cooking time.

Left: Tart ring with parchment circle on non-stick cookie sheet. Right: tart pan, sprayed, with parchment circle.

Preheat your oven to 350°F. Cut a circle of parchment paper to fit the bottom of a non-stick tart pan, preferably with a removable bottom. Spray a little pan spray on the bottom of the pan and stick the parchment to it. Now spray the parchment and the sides of the tart pan with pan spray. Alternatively, use a 9" pastry ring on a non-stick cookie sheet, and spray both. Put the first four ingredients in a mixing bowl, and beat with an electric beater on medium speed for three to four minutes until mixture is light yellow in color and thickened. Add the oil, and beat an additional minute. Now, add the baking powder and the flour, and beat on low until just combined--do not overmix. Add just enough ice water at this point so that the batter resembles thick pancake batter.

Pour the batter into the tart pan and place it in the oven. Bake 15 minutes, then remove from the oven. Use a knife to carefully separate the tart crust's edges from the pan, then slide the knife under the tart crust to separate the parchment paper from the pan. Peel away the parchment paper, and place the crust on a cake rack. Cool five additional minutes, then place the crust on the cake rack back in the oven for five minutes or so, until golden brown. Allow to cool before using.

Do not prefill with custard earlier than 2-3 hours before service or it will be soggy. See strawberry tart, peach or pear tart for recipes with this tart base.

76 calories per serving, 8 slices per tart.

Pâte à Tartelette
TARTLETTE SHELLS

Although this recipe is much lower in calories than the preceding one, and is great for individual tartelettes, it is not useful in my opinion for making a whole tart if the tart crust is to be pre-baked. While such a tart comes out looking well initially, cutting it up into serving portions is a nightmare--the crisp phyllo pastry breaks up and won't cut into pieces properly. You can use it for tarts in which you place a filling and then bake both together, because the phyllo remains damp from the filling, doesn't become as crisp, and therefore will cut as it should.

Serves 12

4	sheets	phyllo dough
		butter-flavored pan spray
8	teaspoons	sugar

Defrost the Phyllo dough in the refrigerator several hours ahead. Follow the directions on the dough package carefully for keeping the dough moist while in use. Prepare to lose a few sheets till you get the hang of it, and don't worry if the sheets tear--just patch 'em up.

Preheat the oven to 350° F. Lay out a single sheet of phyllo dough on a work surface. Spray the sheet all over with pan spray, then sprinkle with 2 teaspoons of the sugar. Repeat with the next sheet, until you have a stack of 4 sheets. Lay a sheet of waxed paper over them, and smooth them down to make them stick together. Using a sharp knife, cut into 12 rectangles.

Lay each rectangle over an individual tartlette pan or mold, and press in place. Trim the edges. Bake 8-12 minutes until golden brown. Remove from the oven, and let cool a few minutes before unmolding. Let them cool completely before use. May be stored in an airtight container at room temperature for about a week, depending on humidity

29 calories per tartlette shell.

For a custard filling, note that one tablespoon of vanilla custard (fat-free, sugar-free) powder is enough to "jell" 1/2 cup of skim milk. That much prepared custard is 70 calories, and will fill at least two tartlettes. Top with fresh berries, paint with melted jelly!

Crème Patisserie et Frangipane
PASTRY CREAM AND FRANGIPANE

These can be used interchangeably. Frangipane is a sort of almond flavored pastry cream.

Serves 8

3 tablespoons sugar
1 1/2 tablespoons cornstarch
1 tablespoon flour
1/2 cup egg substitute such as *Eggbeaters*®
1/2 cup half and half, fat-free

1/3 cup almonds (for Frangipane only, not pastry cream-see below)

Prepare a large mixing bowl with half ice and half water as a water bath. Set a smaller mixing bowl inside, and set aside.

Add the first four ingredients (sugar through egg substitute) to a new mixing bowl, and with an electric mixer beat two to three minutes until light and thick. Meanwhile, place the half and half in a small saucepan, and heat to simmering. Pour about a third of the hot half and half into the egg mixture, whisk, then pour it all back into the saucepan and heat to a simmer while whisking constantly. Occasionally scrape the corners of the pan with a rubber spatula, so the mixture won't burn. When the first signs of bubbling appear, whisk another 30 seconds to a minute and pull the pan off the stove. Immediately pour the custard into the prepared smaller mixing bowl inside the water bath, and stir to cool. When at room temperature, place a piece of saran wrap on top the custard to prevent a skim from forming, and refrigerate.

To make frangipane, add 1/4 teaspoon of almond extract and a third of a cup of ground almonds (if no ground almonds handy, use slivered or whole blanched and grind with a few pulses of the food processor). Frangipane is used like pastry cream in tarts that are to be baked, where you want a tasty almond flavor (see for example Tarte ou Frangipane aux Pêches ou Abricots).

44 calories per serving when divided into eight portions for the pastry cream;
58 calories per serving for the frangipane.

Sauces

What defines French cooking? Is there an essence to it that can be distilled so that all may know it? Perhaps it is an oversimplification to say that sauce is the answer, but certainly sauces are a part of the foundation upon which French cooking is based.

The word sauce is derived from the Latin salsus, meaning "to salt". Historically, marinating in salt was required because refrigeration was nonexistent. The brine in which meat, fish and poultry were preserved was often used in ancient times in cooking a dish and to accompany it. Because meat was not available in abundance, it was traditional to serve bread with the meal to sop up these juices, and one could conclude that the original thickening of these liquids was accomplished with bread.

In Charlemagne's time, according to David Paul Larousse in, "The Sauce Bible," a dodine was a sauce made by rubbing toasted, seasoned bread through a sieve, placing it under a roast, and then serving it with the dish. He further explains that in the fourteenth century, a distinction was made between *sauce* and *grané*. While sauce was a thickened, seasoned, brew of a liquid, grané was a meat stew thickened with grains. Our *gravy* is apparently a corruption of grané.

In the seventeenth century, a more systematic approach to sauces and gravies was developed by Antoine Carême. He divided the sauces into four groupings--Espagnole, velouté, Allemande and béchamel. This was the basis from which "the French sauce system" we know today was begun. Escoffier revised the categories, naming the basics in the mid-nineteenth century the "mother sauces" from which many other sauces are derived. These are, from his *Guide Culinaire* (1902): 1)sauce tomate (red sauce), 2) béchamel (cream or white sauce), 3)velouté (blond sauce), 4)the butter sauces, Hollandaise and Béarnaise, and 5)Espagnole (brown sauce).

In this book you will find my recipes for *every one* of these classic "mother sauces" of French cooking, especially created to allow you to integrate them into your diet with ease. This opens tremendous possibilities, because you could make a hundred dishes, all different, with the sauces listed below. No recipe is required--you can be your own chef! All you need to do is match up a tasty sauce with any reasonable portion of meat, chicken or fish, prepared in a simple fashion such as poached, sautéed, or grilled, and you'll have so many possibilities you won't need the rest of the cookbook. I've given some examples of traditional pairings, such as the Nantua Sauce with Quenelles, and I have suggested some of the more customary uses of some of the sauces, but often I've left it wide open. Some great and innovative pairings are yours to discover!

With the exception of the tomato and possibly the Espagnole sauces, none of the sauces can be successfully brought to boiling without ruining them. Heat and reheat only to *just below a simmer*. The butter sauces, in particular, are traditionally served *tiède*, that is, warm. Do not overheat them!

1. FRENCH-STYLE TOMATO SAUCE

There are many, many uses for tomato sauce, as you already know. Consider using it as the French would, cold to accompany an aspic, hot with poached or grilled fish, or with steamed shrimp over pasta. See the stuffed mussels recipe for a special preparation.

Serves 6

    2   tablespoons   olive oil
    1   shallot -- minced
    1   medium onion -- finely diced
    2   cloves garlic -- minced
    2   tablespoons flour
    2   beef bouillon cubes
    1   28 ounce can   tomatoes, peeled and seeded
    1   teaspoon sugar
    2   sprigs   thyme
    2   bay leaves

Cook the onion, shallot and garlic in the olive oil on medium, covered, about five to ten minutes until softened but not brown. Add the flour; stir and cook until flour begins to brown. Add one cup water, tomatoes, and all remaining ingredients. Bring to a simmer, and cook uncovered, stirring occasionally, for 45 minutes. Remove the thyme and bay leaf, and purée in a food processor. Some prefer to strain through a food mill. Season with salt and pepper.

75 calories per 1/2 cup serving.

2. SAUCE BÉCHAMEL AND ITS VARIATIONS

In making these sauces, I opted in the recipe for the lowest possible calorie count, therefore choosing 1% milk as the basis for the sauce (skim milk is really unpalatable in these sauces—to me). Following the relative value chart for creams and milks, found under "basics", you may choose to try for example fat- free half and half in place of 1% milk. This will improve the taste--at a cost--of course. But not all of you need to be at 800 calories per day, so you decide!

Serves 8

1	medium onion
3	whole cloves
2	tablespoons butter
1/4	cup flour
2	cups 1% lowfat milk
1/2	bay leaf
1/2	teaspoon salt
1	pinch white pepper
1	pinch nutmeg

Stud the onion with the cloves, and set it aside for a moment. Melt butter in a heavy saucepan. Remove from heat and stir in the flour. Place back over medium-low heat, stir slowly and cook about one minute. Do not allow to color. Add the milk, the studded onion, and the bay leaf, and cook on low heat (below a simmer) about 15 to 20 minutes. Stir regularly during the cooking. Discard the onion, cloves and bay leaf. Season with salt, nutmeg, and white pepper.

64 calories per quarter cup serving.

Variations:

2.1 Sauce Mornay

Cheese sauce: add 1/4 cup grated lowfat Swiss cheese (74 calories)

2.2 Sauce Nantua

Crayfish sauce: simmer 1/4 cup diced crayfish tails in 1/2 cup water, and fry their shells, finely cracked, in two tablespoons of butter. Strain the shells, add to the diced tails, reduce till the water's gone, add 2 cups béchamel sauce. Try with Quenelles, see recipe. Note: leave a few crayfish whole as a garnish (96 calories).

2.3 Sauce Soubise

Onion sauce: cook 2 cups diced onions in 1 cup water until 3/4 done. Drain, discarding water. Cook onions in 1 tablespoons butter in non-stick fry pan until soft. Add 2 cups béchamel sauce, stirring and cooking 2 minutes. Strain, discarding onions. Bring to a simmer and add 1/2 cup half and half and juice of 1/2 lemon. Season with salt and pepper (92 calories per 1/4 cup).

2.4 Sauce Cardinal

Lobster sauce: add 1/4 cup cooked minced lobster meat, 2 tablespoons butter, 1/4 cup half and half, and 1 tablespoons minced truffles (failing to find truffles in the cupboard, consider minced wild mushrooms) (106 calories).

2.5 Sauce Ecossaise

Scotch egg sauce: Add three diced hard-cooked eggs and season with nutmeg (88 calories).

3. SAUCE VELOUTÉ AND ITS VARIATIONS

Serves 8

2	tablespoons	butter
2	tablespoons	flour
2	cups fish stock or chicken stock (do you want fish velouté or chicken velouté?)	
1	teaspoon cornstarch	

Melt the butter in a 1 quart saucepan. Add the flour slowly, whisking to incorporate. Turn the heat to low, and continue whisking and cooking 2-3 minutes. If the roux threatens to brown, pull it off the heat for a minute. Add the stock, and turn up the heat to bring the sauce to a lazy simmer. Continue whisking, off and on, until thickened. If the sauce is not sufficiently thick to coat the back of a spoon, make a slurry by mixing the cornstarch with 2 tablespoons of water, and whisk it in. Occasionally, it has taken two teaspoons of cornstarch. Continue cooking and stirring until thickened. Season with salt and pepper.

59 calories per 1/4 cup serving.

The following variations are for velouté made with fish stock, and are good with any poached fish.

3.1 Sauce Dieppoise

Shrimp and Mussel Sauce: Add 1/3 cup shelled cooked mussels, 6 cooked peeled and minced shrimp (71 calories).

3.2 Sauce Homard

Lobster Sauce: Add 1 teaspoons paprika, 1/2 cup cooked diced lobster meat (71 calories).

3.3 Sauce Safran

Saffron Sauce: Take a healthy pinch of saffron and grind it in a mortar and pestle (or mince it with a knife—but the mortar and pestle brings out the saffron flavor better). Add to the velouté (59 calories).

3.4 Sauce Fines Herbes

Herb Sauce: Add a tablespoon each of chopped shallots, parsley, chervil and chives (61 calories).

The following are intended for velouté made with chicken stock:

3.5 Sauce Aurore I

Aurora Sauce I: Add two tablespoons of tomato paste (68 calories per quarter cup serving).

3.6 Sauce Suprême

Suprême Sauce: Add 3 ounces half and half (73 calories).

Two Variations on Sauce Suprême: for poultry egg and fish dishes

3.61 Sauce Aurore II

Aurora Sauce II: Add one-half cup of prepared tomato sauce (see recipe or use something comparable to Ragú Lite), strain before serving (79 calories).

3.62 Sauce Ivoire

Ivory sauce: Add beef bouillon enough to give the sauce an ivory color (60 calories).

3.7 Sauce Bercy

Sauce Bercy: Cook a tablespoon of minced shallots in 1/2 cup white wine and 1/2 cup fish stock (see recipe), boil to reduce to one-half cup. Add 1 cup velouté sauce, and bring to just below simmering, then remove from the heat. Swirl in 2 tablespoons butter and a tablespoon of chopped parsley. Delightful with fish(102 calories).

4. The Butter Sauces

Note: In making the butter and egg sauces Hollandaise and Béarnaise, I strongly recommend that you use pasteurized egg substitute such as *Eggbeaters®* rather than whole eggs. The eggs in these recipes are not sufficiently cooked to kill salmonella, a potentially toxic bacteria found in some areas of the country.

4.1 Hollandaise Sauce

Serves 4

2   tablespoons butter
1   cup chicken stock
2   tablespoons lemon juice
    white pepper
1/2 cup egg substitute

Melt butter on 50% power in microwave for 1 to 2 minutes until liquid. Set aside. Add the lemon juice and chicken stock to a saucepan, season with salt and white pepper, and reduce to 2/3 cup. Meanwhile, pour the egg substitute into a one quart saucepan, and attach a candy thermometer to its side (if you have no candy thermometer, you'll have to be especially careful of the heat in this next step, so as not to end up with scrambled eggs).

When the stock is reduced, whisk the eggs over low heat while very slowly adding the hot stock, a little at a time. Watch carefully and remove the sauce from the fire when it thickens to the consistency of heavy cream--about 120° to 125°F. This should take 2 or 3 minutes. Immediately pour into a food processor, and with the processor running, drizzle in the melted butter.

If the sauce is to be used immediately, let it stand about 5 minutes before serving. Otherwise, pour it into a wide mouth thermos and it will keep an hour while you prepare the rest of the meal. You can refrigerate the sauce; reheat it for 30 seconds at 50% power in the microwave, or *very* gently on the stove.

74 calories per quarter cup serving.

4.11 Curry Hollandaise

Add one to two teaspoons of curry powder to the finished one cup of Hollandaise. Serve on fish, shellfish, and eggs (74 calories).

4.12 Sauce Figaro

To one cup of Hollandaise, add 3 tablespoons tomato sauce, 1 teaspoon tomato paste, 2 teaspoons minced parsley and cayenne pepper to taste (77 calories).

4.13 Sauce Mousseline

For that extra-special occasion, fold 1/4 cup whipped heavy cream into one cup Hollandaise. Heavenly on fish (125 calories per serving)!

4.2 Béarnaise Sauce

Béarnaise sauce was created in the early part of the nineteenth century by the chef of the restaurant Pavillon Henry IV, in Saint-Germain-en-Laye just outside Paris. The sauce was created in fact for King Henry IV, "the Great Béarnais," for whom the restaurant was named. If you see a dish prepared today labeled "Henri IV" it means Béarnaise sauce mixed with meat juice.

Béarnaise sauce is most often served nowadays with a piece of the tenderloin which has been grilled or roasted, a tradition begun by Montmireil, chef to the Vicomte of Chateaubriand. It goes equally well with any grilled, sautéed or roasted meat, and its uses have been expanded to include chicken and fish as well. See recipe for Chateaubriand à la Béarnaise.

Serves 4

2	tablespoons	butter
3	tablespoons	white wine vinegar (or tarragon vinegar)
1	tablespoon	shallots -- minced
		peppercorns -- cracked
1/2	cup white wine	
1/2	cup chicken stock	
1/2	cup egg substitute	
2	teaspoons tarragon -- dried	

Melt butter on 50% power in microwave for 1 to 2 minutes until liquid. Set aside. Add the vinegar, shallots, pepper, white wine, and chicken stock to a saucepan, and reduce to 2/3 cup. Meanwhile, pour the egg substitute into a one-quart saucepan and attach a candy thermometer to its side (if you have no candy thermometer, you'll have to be especially careful of the heat in this next step so as not to end up with scrambled eggs).

Strain the vinegar reduction when it is finished. While whisking the eggs over low heat, slowly add the reduction, a little at a time. Watch carefully and remove the sauce from the fire when it thickens to the consistency of heavy cream--about 120° to 125°F. This should take 2 or 3 minutes. Immediately pour into a food processor, and with the processor running, drizzle in the melted butter. Add the tarragon, and let stand about 5 minutes before serving (it will thicken slightly). Alternatively, keep warm in a wide mouth vacuum bottle, or refrigerate and reheat for 30 seconds on 50% power in the microwave.

83 calories per quarter cup serving.

4.21 Sauce Choron

To one cup of Béarnaise, add two tablespoons tomato purée, and omit the herbs. Serve with grilled meats (86 calories).

4.3 Beurre Blanc

    2 shallots -- or 1 small red onion
    1/2 cup white wine
          pinch of white pepper
    1 teaspoon cornstarch
    7 tablespoons butter

Peel and chop the shallots. Pour the wine into a saucepan, add the shallots and cook over moderately high heat until reduced to about one ounce. Strain and discard the shallots. Return the liquid to the saucepan, season with salt and white pepper, and whisk in the cornstarch carefully to avoid lumps. After reheating to the simmering point, add one tablespoon of the butter and whisk in. Lower the heat to low and add the butter, one tablespoon at a time, whisking constantly, until all the butter is incorporated.

See Salmon in a Dill Beurre Blanc

5. SAUCE ESPAGNOLE AND ITS VARIATIONS

Serves 8

    2 tablespoons butter
    1/4 cup carrots -- minced
    1/4 cup celery -- minced
    1/2 cup onions -- minced
    4 tablespoons flour
    1 tablespoon sugar
    1/2 cup red wine

3 cups beef stock (or chicken stock, or veal stock)
1/2 teaspoon brown seasoning sauce such as Kitchen Bouquet (optional but recommended)
1/2 bay leaf
1/2 teaspoon thyme -- dried
2 tablespoons tomato paste

Melt the butter in a large sauté pan on low heat, and add the minced vegetables (items two through four), cooking slowly and stirring, until vegetables are softened, about five minutes. Mix the flour and sugar, and sprinkle over the vegetables. Continue cooking over low heat another ten minutes or so, until the vegetables appear to be brown--almost, but not quite to the the point of burning. Turn the heat up to medium, add the wine, allow to reduce a minute or two, and add the beef stock and the seasoning sauce, the bay leaf and the thyme. Bring to a boil, then simmer about 20 to 30 minutes until reduced to 2 1/4 cups. Strain, add the tomato paste, and season with salt and pepper.

Note: If the sauce is too thick, dilute with beef stock. If the sauce is too thin, you can use it as it is in another recipe (for example Sauce Chasseur) and the thicken the final product with a slurry of water and cornstarch. If you try to thicken it now, and then reheat it to a simmer, the thickening power of the cornstarch will be much reduced.

63 calories per quarter cup serving.

5.1 Sauce Chasseur

Serves 8

1	cup	mushrooms -- sliced
1	small	onion -- minced
1/2	cup	chicken stock
1/2	cup	white wine
1	cup	Sauce Espagnole
1/2	teaspoon	tarragon -- dried
2	tablespoons	tomato paste
1/2	teaspoon	parsley -- chopped

Add the sliced mushrooms and minced onions to a one quart saucepan, add the chicken stock and the white wine, and set the pan on medium-high heat. Allow the liquid to boil until it is almost gone, and only a thick syrup remains. Add the Sauce Espagnole, the tarragon, the tomato paste and the parsley and bring to a simmer. Season with salt and pepper, and if too thin, whisk in one tablespoon of cornstarch dissolved in a tablespoon or two of water.

57 calories per quarter cup serving

5.2 Sauce Robert

Serves 6

1	small	onion -- minced
1/2	cup	white wine
2	tablespoons	white wine vinegar
1 1/4	cups	Sauce Espagnole
2	tablespoons	tomato paste
1	tablespoon	mustard
1	teaspoon	parsley -- dried

Add the onion, the white wine, and the white wine vinegar to a one quart saucepan, bring to a boil and reduce the liquid by three-quarters. Add the Sauce Espagnole and the tomato paste, simmer five minutes. Add the mustard and parsley, season with salt and pepper, and adjust the consistency as for the sauces above.

78 calories per quarter cup serving.

5.3 Sauce Madeira

Serves 4

1	small	onion -- minced
1/2	cup	Madeira (or port or sherry)
1	cup	Sauce Espagnole

Add the onion and the Madeira to a one quart saucepan, and bring to a boil. Simmer until the Madeira is reduced almost completely (a thick glaze in the bottom of the pan), then add the Sauce Espagnole and bring up to a simmer. Thicken if necessary as above.

114 calories per quarter cup serving.

MINOR SAUCES

Sauce Albert

Horseradish Sauce

Serves 4

8	ounces	chicken stock
2	teaspoons	butter
1	tablespoon	flour
1	tablespoon	horseradish -- grated, prepared
2	teaspoons	mustard
1/4	cup	half and half

Bring the chicken stock to a simmer. Knead the butter and flour together to make a beurre manié. Add bit by bit to the simmering stock, stirring, until thickened. Add the horseradish and mustard, then season with salt and pepper. Add the half and half, remove from the heat, and blend thoroughly. Serve with boiled, roast or braised beef, duck, tuna. See Magret de Canard recipe.
56 calories per serving.

Sauce Au Curry

CURRY SAUCE

Serves 4

1/2	cup chicken stock
1	teaspoon butter, softened
1	teaspoon flour
1/2	teaspoon curry powder (or to taste)
1	teaspoon mustard
2	tablespoons sour cream, light

Bring the chicken stock to a simmer. Make a paste of the butter and flour (beurre manié), and add it little by little, whisking, until the sauce thickens. Add the curry and mustard, then season with salt and pepper. Remove from the heat, and whisk in the sour cream. Serve hot.
Great with sliced hot breast of chicken!

19 calories per quarter cup serving.

Sauce notes: With some of the recipes, you may wish to try a prepared sauce. Although there is *frequently a calorie saving with these sauces, the taste is often poor. The only packaged prepared dry sauces I think are worthwhile (amongst those I have come across), are the Maggi "Cuisine Française" sauces. They come in 7 ounce packets to serve 3, reconstitute with water, and have about 30-35 calories per serving.*

SALAD DRESSING

Sauce Moutarde pour la Salade

MUSTARD VINAIGRETTE FOR SALAD

Serves 8
- 1/4 cup safflower oil
- 1/4 cup white wine vinegar
- 1/8 cup Dijon mustard
- 1   teaspoon sugar
- 1/2 teaspoon sesame oil

Pour everything in the blender, and turn it on high. It's done!
68 calories per tablespoon.

OTHER SAUCES

ROUILLE
("roo-EE")

For how to use, see Ragôut des Poissons Provençal (Provençal Fish Stew).
Serves 6

- 1/2   cup roasted red peppers, diced (or drained canned peppers or pimentos)
- 1/2   teaspoon red wine vinegar
- 2   large garlic cloves minced
- 1/2   cup mayonnaise, lowfat (divided)
         hot pepper sauce to taste

Add roasted pepper, vinegar, and garlic to the bowl of a food processor and process until smooth. Add 1/4 cup mayonnaise and pulse until just combined. Transfer to a small bowl, add remaining mayonnaise, season with salt, pepper, and hot pepper sauce to taste. Mix well. Refrigerate at least 30 minutes before serving.

23 calories per serving.

CHAUD-FROID SAUCE
("show-FWAH" sauce)

1 3/4 cups chicken stock   (divided)
1   package unflavored gelatin
1/4   cup half and half

This sauce is used in the preparation of aspics. It is a white liquid that you pour or brush on a cold meats or poultry, and when refrigerated thereafter it firms up into a white jelly which can then be decorated. It can be dyed with food color to permit very creative displays for a buffet, for example. It can be diced, or cut into shapes and laid over cold meats or fish. It's very simple to make.

Bring half the chicken stock to boiling, add and dissolve the gelatin. Pour in the rest of the stock and the half and half, and chill until cold but not set. Ready for use. 22 calories per quarter cup.

DESSERT SAUCES
Coulis aux Framboise
RASPBERRY SAUCE

Serves 6

10   ounces   raspberries -- frozen, thawed
1   teaspoon   cornstarch
1/4   cup sugar -- to taste

Puree raspberries in food processor, then strain through a chinois or sieve, or puree with a food mill. Scrape any pulp clinging to underside of sieve. Add cornstarch to 2 tablespoons of mixture, return mixture to saucepan and add raspberries. Simmer over medium-high heat, adding sugar until just slightly thickened and clear. Chill, stores 3 or 4 days. Makes 3/4 cup, or six 2-tablespoon servings.   56 calories per 2 tablespoon serving.

Crème Anglaise
VANILLA CUSTARD SAUCE

I have tested at least ten variations on low-cal Crème Anglaise, all made from scratch. None tastes better, and all are higher in calories and fat than this simple interpretation.
Serves 6

1 1/2 tablespoons   vanilla pudding mix, instant -- no-fat, no-sugar, such as *Jello®*
1 1/2 cups skim milk

Whip ingredients together with electric mixer two minutes, then chill. Ready for use in ten minutes or tomorrow. If the Crème Anglais thickens too much in the refrigerator, thin with a little skim milk and re-whip.

See Coulis aux Framboises, and Soufflé Grand Marnier.

20 calories per quarter cup serving.

Appetizers, Soups, and Luncheons

Tomates Maison
HOME-STYLE TOMATOES

Serves 4

4   large tomatoes
4   tablespoons chèvre (goat cheese), room temperature
        lettuce
1   sprig fresh parsley
        salad dressing

Using the best tomatoes you can find, cut the top off the tomatoes, and stand them up on this flat end. Using a very sharp knife, remove long narrow slices of tomato, but don't cut all the way to the bottom. Fill each newly created space with small bits of the goat cheese. Wipe off any cheese that gets on the surface of the tomato. The tomato should have a red and white striped appearance.

Place the tomato on a bed of lettuce leaves, and sprinkle the parsley on top. A little salad dressing finishes the dish.

55 calories each.

Crudités à la Sauce aux Anchois
CRUDITÉS IN ANCHOVY SAUCE

Serves 4

For the Sauce:

1   2 oz. can anchovy fillets -- (about 6 fillets)
10   capers
1   small onion -- roughly chopped
1   clove garlic -- roughly chopped
4   sprigs parsley -- roughly chopped
1/4   teaspoon herbs de Provence
6   tablespoons   Marie's Fat-free Classic Herb Vinaigrette
        For the Crudités -- for example:
                baby carrots, radishes,celery, broccoli florets, cauliflower florets, and mush-
rooms.

Add all the sauce ingredients to a blender. Purée.
Serve as a dipping sauce for the crudités.

Making a homemade sauce or dressing is easy, but making one in which the calorie count rivals the lowfat or no-fat dressings you can buy commercially, and yet still has taste, is very, very hard. I think this one combines the best of both worlds. Using the no-fat dressing as a base instead of oil keep the count down, and using fresh ingredients gives a really homemade taste! It can also be used as a salad dressing.

About 55 calories each for four one-ounce servings of dip, plus the crudités.

Tomates Farcies au Caille de Brebis
TOMATOES STUFFED WITH CHÈVRE (GOAT CHEESE)

Try these for a crowd---inexpensive, low-cal and tasty !
Recipe by Chef Jean Bardet, of Jean Bardet, Tours
Serves 40

40	small	tomatoes (not cherry tomatoes)
1		onion
1		zucchini
1		eggplant
1		green pepper
1		red pepper
3	ounces	olive oil
2	ounces	basil, fresh
1	cup	half and half
1	pound	chèvre cheese
1	cup	tomato juice

Preheat the oven to 350°F. Cut a "hat" off the top of each tomato, leaving the stalk, if you're lucky enough to get farm tomatoes, intact. Reserve the hat for later. Scoop out the seeds, and season with pepper, and especially with salt. Try not to remove the inner separations, as the tomatoes may fall apart when baked. Invert the tomatoes on absorbent toweling to drain. Mince the onion, zucchini, eggplant, and peppers, then sauté them in the olive oil. Drain them and reserve. Finely chop the basil. Boil the light cream until reduced by half, and add the basil. Mix the chèvre with the cream and the minced sautéed vegetables, and stuff the tomatoes. Cover with the hat. Arrange on a baking dish, and add a cup of tomato juice in the bottom of the dish. Bake 15 minutes. Serve garnished with small basil leaves, and a little of the cooking juice.

See all about Jean Bardet under the recipe for "Gratin de Blettes a la Brebis du Lochois".
84 calories per serving (one tomato).

Tomates Cerises Farcies
STUFFED CHERRY TOMATOES

If it's only family, instead of a crowd, you might want an ultra-simple version for a very low-cal appetizer, say, with a martini at cocktail time. These are practically devoid of calories, and yet they satisfy!

Serves 4
12 cherry tomatoes
1/3 cup fat free ranch dip (or onion soup mix with fat-free sour cream)

Carefully cut off the top of each tomato, leaving the little stem intact. Reserve the tops. With a teaspoon, gently scoop out the seeds and dividing membranes inside. Fill each of the tomato shells with about a teaspoon of dip. Affix each lid at a jaunty angle, and serve.
41 calories for three stuffed cherry tomatoes.

Potage Purée de Cresson
PURÉE OF WATERCRESS SOUP

This is a great way to use up leftover watercress. It makes a tasty soup, which is easy to prepare, and which won't be hard to fit into the day's calorie budget.

Serves 6
1   bunch watercress
2   tablespoons butter
2   large onions -- peeled & chopped
2   large potatoes -- peeled & chopped
3   cups chicken stock
3   tablespoons sour cream, light

Reserve a few leaves of the watercress for each portion for garnish. Boil some water, salt it, and add the leaves of watercress. Cook one or two minutes, then plunge into cold water and drain. Chop the rest of the watercress roughly. Melt the butter in a sautoir over a medium heat, and add the onions. Sauté until they become transparent, then add the chopped watercress, the potatoes and the stock. Bring to a boil, then reduce the heat and simmer 20 minutes or so until the potatoes are cooked. Add one-third of the contents of the sautoir to a food processor, and pulse until puréed. Add the rest of the vegetables from the pot, again pulsing until puréed. Finally, add the liquid and the sour cream, and once again purée. Season with salt. Divide the soup into six pre-heated soup plates, garnish with the blanched watercress leaves, and serve. For an extra few calories, you can add an additional tablespoon of light sour cream in the center of each soup plate as garnish (if desired).
88 calories per serving.

Soupe à la Tomate
TOMATO SOUP

Serves 4

    1 1/2 pounds tomatoes -- quartered*
    2 slices bacon
    1/2 cup carrots -- diced
    1 small onion -- chopped
    10 ounces chicken stock (canned or your own--see recipe)
    1 teaspoon sugar
    1 tablespoon parsley -- flat, chopped

Pass the tomatoes through the medium blade of a food mill. Then, cook the bacon with carrots and onions, stirring frequently, until the bacon has browned. Remove and discard the bacon. Add the tomatoes and chicken stock, season with salt and pepper. Bring to boil, then turn down the heat and simmer 30 minutes. Pass the whole soup through the fine blade of the food mill. Add the sugar, reheat, check the seasoning and serve in preheated bowls. Garnish with the chopped parsley.

*As an alternative to fresh tomatoes, use canned whole tomatoes out of season. Substitute a rib of celery for the carrots, and 1 tablespoon of butter for the bacon. Or, add 1/4 cup fat-free half-and-half to the completed soup and serve over a tablespoon of cooked rice.
81 calories.

Aspics de Poulet aux Légumes
CHICKEN AND VEGETABLES IN ASPIC

Serves 4

    1 pound chicken breasts without skin -- chopped, cooked
    1 cup chicken stock
    1 cup vermouth
    2 cups vegetables, mixed -- frozen thawed
    2 packets unflavored gelatin -- unsweetened
    1/2 cup mayonnaise, lowfat
    1 tablespoon chervil

This is a wonderful recipe for leftovers, and can be made with any leftover cooked meat or fish.

Bring the chicken stock to a boil in a saucepan, and add the vegetables, simmering until they are cooked. Mix the unflavored gelatin powder with the cold vermouth, and add it and the chicken to the pot. Bring to a boil, then allow to cool slightly. Pour into a one quart loaf pan or terrine lined with plastic wrap. Press down the meat and vegetables so that they are just under the level of the liquid. Refrigerate. Mix the mayonnaise with the chervil. When the aspic is completely set, slice and serve with 2 tablespoons of herbed mayonnaise.

Serving Ideas : Consider a small salad with vinaigrette on the side.

299 calories.

Moules à la Sauce Verte
MUSSELS IN AN HERB MAYONNAISE

Serves 2

2	dozen mussels	
1	teaspoon	parsley
2	teaspoons	dill
1	clove	garlic
1/4	cup mayonnaise, low fat	

Wash and clean the mussels thoroughly. Discard any whose shells don't close after tapping them. Steam the mussels in a steamer basket for five minutes, then spread them out on a plate and allow them to cool in the refrigerator. Chop the parsley and the dill finely, and mix in a small bowl with the garlic and the mayonnaise. Then put the herb mayonnaise in a small plastic "baggy", eject the air and tie the top. Snip off a tiny corner of the bag, and pipe the herb mayonnaise onto the cold mussels. Serve a dozen mussels each, for example with a mesclun salad in vinaigrette.

Also makes a lovely first course, but decrease the portion size to 6-8 mussels per person!

164 calories per portion.

Rillettes de Tours
RILLETTES

("re-YET")

Serves 4

Rillettes are traditionally made from pork cooked with and mixed into its own fat, seasoned with salt, pepper and herbs. Rillettes are made commercially all over France, and often sold tinned. They are commonly spread on ficelle or baguettes and eaten for lunch, but they do well on rounds of French bread or crackers as a wonderful appetizer. The best rillettes in France comes from Tours in the Loire Valley, and good rillettes all over France are commonly called Rillettes de Tours.

In an attempt to lighten the heavy calorie count of rillettes, without losing all the taste, I finally found a good use for that otherwise tasteless stuff called fat-free margarine. For once, it isn't the fat I want to taste, and the bland flavor of fat-free margarine is an acceptable vehicle for the pork and seasonings. It would also work with shrimp to make a decent and VERY low-cal shrimp butter.

1/2	pound	pork tenderloin
1	whole	clove
1		bay leaf
1/2	cup	boiling water
4	tablespoons	Fat-freee margarine
1	pinch	marjoram
1	pinch	sage -- dried
1	pinch	rosemary
1	pinch	black pepper
1		baguette

Cube the pork tenderloin, add the clove and bay leaf, and boil in the water just until cooked through. Remove the clove

Rillettes de porc for sale in a charcuterie in Tours

and bay leaf and drain well. Pass through the food processor until finely minced, then remove to a mixing bowl and chill. When cold, mix in the remaining ingredients(margarine through black pepper), and chill again. Slice the baguette into 4 pieces, and spread each with 1/4 of the meat mixture. Serve with a cup of soup or a little salad for a delicious lunch.

As shown 290 calories per person. About 30 calories per tablespoon; average portion is about 90 calories, plus the baguette.

Œufs Pochés en Berceau
EGGS POACHED IN THE CRADLE

Serves 4

4		potatoes such as Idahoes
1	cup	Sauce Aurore (see recipe)
8		eggs
1/2	cup	cooked chicken -- diced
1/4	cup	mayonnaise, lowfat
1/8	cup	onion -- diced
1/8	cup	celery -- diced
1	pinch	parsley
		sliced tomatoes & salad for garnish

Bake the potatoes in the oven, and while they are baking prepare Sauce Aurore according to the directions under variations of Béchamel sauce. Place it in a vacuum bottle to keep it hot. When the potatoes are done, skin them, halve them, and cut out the center to remove the pulp. They will resembles little "cradles" at this point ("berceau", in French). Keep them hot. Poach the eggs according to the instructions under basic preparations (Œufs Pochés), omitting the bread. Keep them hot, or rewarm at service time by placing them in a fry pan with 1/4" of water and bringing to a simmer. Mix the next 5 ingredients (chicken through parsley), and fill each potato with a little of the mixture. Place a poached egg on top, and ladle about 2 tablespoons of sauce over each. Garnish with the salad and tomatoes.

318 calories.

Œufs Pochés Mornay
POACHED EGGS MORNAY

Serves 4

1	cup	sauce Mornay (see recipe)
8		eggs
8		bread slices, low-cal
1/4	cup	bread crumbs
1/4	cup	Swiss cheese, lowfat -- grated

Follow the recipe for the Mornay sauce (sauces), and for poaching eggs (œufs pochés under basic preparations). Set the eggs on the rounds of bread, and spoon two tablespoons of Mornay sauce over each egg. Then sprinkle with both bread crumbs and Swiss cheese. Give a quick spray to each with butter flavored pan spray, and place under broiler just until cheese melts. Serve hot.

320 calories.

Œufs à la Bourguignonne

EGGS POACHED BURGUNDY STYLE

Serves 4

1 cup red wine
1 cup chicken stock
8 eggs
1 clove garlic -- minced
1 bay leaf
1/4 teaspoon thyme -- dried
1/2 cup onions -- chopped
2 whole duck or chicken livers
1 teaspoon butter
1 cup mushrooms -- sliced
8 slices of bread, low-cal
1 teaspoon cornstarch
1 tablespoon currant jelly
2 tablespoons butter
fresh chervil for garnish

Place the wine and the chicken stock in a small frypan (about 8"--this becomes important), and bring to a boil. Turn the heat down to just below a simmer, so that the liquid stops bubbling. Break the eggs into cups, and slide them into the poaching liquid (see directions for poached eggs under Basics). Do this in two batches. Poach 3 to 5 minutes, remove to a cutting board, and trim ragged edges. Slide the eggs into a non-stick fry pan in which you've poured just enough poaching liquid to cover the bottom of the pan, and set aside. To the rest of the poaching liquid add the garlic, bay leaf, thyme and onions, and boil rapidly down to 1 cup. Strain, and keep simmering.   Sauté the duck livers in one teaspoon of butter in a non-stick sauté pan. Slice the livers on a diagonal, season with salt and pepper, and keep warm. Boil the mushrooms till soft; drain and reserve. Toast the bread and use a biscuit cutter or cookie cutter to cut a circle out of each slice of toast. Discard the crust, reserving the rounds of toast. Make a slurry of the cornstarch with two tablespoons of cold water, and stir it into the simmering poaching liquid, to thicken. Add the mushrooms, currant jelly, and season with salt and pepper. Place the pan with the eggs on low heat until the water simmers, remove the eggs one at a time with a slotted spoon, and then place each on a toast round set on a pre-heated plate. Place the livers around the plate.   Whisk the two tablespoons of butter into the mushroom-wine sauce off the heat at the last minute, and ladle over and around the eggs and livers. Garnish with the chervil, and serve hot.

349 calories, with the duck livers.   *Serve it with some cooked spinach on the side.*

Œufs en Gelée

EGGS IN ASPIC

This dish is my all time favorite for an appetizer or light lunch. It looks very festive, has endless variations, is simple to prepare, and is low in calories!

The term "aspic" refers to a dish made with a gelée of meat, fish or poultry, not actually to the jelly itself, while "gelée" can mean either. The variation presented here is only one of many, as a suggestion. Consider, for example, replacing the poached egg with a small amount of salmon or chicken mousse (see recipe) piped into the mold, the shrimp with country ham, adding cooked asparagus tips or sliced carrots, etc. You can cover any of the ingredients with Chaud-Froid Sauce (see recipe) prior to including it in the aspic, or use the Chaud-Froid sauce as a bottom layer for a different effect. You can prepare these as individual servings, as done here, or as a large single mold. I have seen a lovely presentation of poached eggs and sliced truffles in a ring mold to serve six *(when you make this one, let me know, so I can come for dinner!)*.

Serves 8

3 1/2	cups	clarified chicken stock -- see below*
1/2	cup	Madeira -- sherry or Vermouth
2	packages	unflavored gelatin
1	6 oz. can	medium whole shrimp (or better yet, fresh boiled)
4		eggs
		parsley, yellow & red peppers for garnish

*This dish is most attractive when the stock is clarified, but it is not essential. To clarify the stock, mix together 1/4 cup chopped celery stalk, 1/4 cup chopped carrot, 1/4 cup chopped onion, and 4 egg whites with the cold stock. Bring to a simmer, whisking gently just enough to keep the egg whites dispersed. When the mixture reaches a simmer, stop stirring. Now, keep the mixture at barely a simmer about 10 minutes. Strain the liquid through a sieve lined with cheesecloth. Do not press down on the solids or they will cloud the clarified stock.

Bring half the chicken stock to a boil, add and dissolve the gelatin, then remove from the stove and add the remaining stock and Madeira. Pour about 2 tablespoons of aspic in the bottoms of each of eight half-cup molds (custard cups work) and place in the refrigerator until set. Begin to chill the remaining jelly as well, but do not let it set. Meanwhile, cut a small, fairly flat section from each pepper and cut into strips about 1/2" wide. Trim away all but about 1/4" of pepper flesh under the skin, and cut these strips into 1/2" diamond shapes, or any shape you prefer. Lay them, alternating colors, skin side down, on top of the set jelly, pour a thin layer of new jelly over these and let them set.

Start the eggs in cold water, bring them to a boil, and boil them for about 7 minutes, then place them in the refrigerator to chill. When the last layer of jelly has set, arrange the shrimp on top, and pour a new layer. Chill. When set, put in half an egg, yolk side down (so that when you invert the mold it will be yolk side up), and fill the rest of the mold with jelly. Refrigerate several hours until well set. To unmold, dip the molds in hot water briefly and invert on a luncheon plate on which you have arranged some greens. Serve cold with lowfat mayonnaise spooned or piped on or around the aspic (the mayo can go in a baggie, eject the air, seal the bag, snip off the corner, and squeeze to pipe). Or serve with mustard vinaigrette spooned on the plate and drizzled over the greens. Or with cold tomato sauce. Garnish with gherkins, olives, chopped tomatoes, radishes, etc.

99 calories each serving.

Les Oeufs Casino

EGGS CASINO

Serves 6

1/3 cup		Chaud-Froid sauce -- see recipe
2 drops		red food coloring
13		eggs
6		tartlette shells
1/2 cup		cooked chicken -- diced
6		asparagus tips -- cooked
3 tablespoons		mayonnaise, lowfat
6 slices		ham slices, extra lean
4		black olives

Lovely as an appetizer for a small buffet, or as a first course where the main course is low in calories.

Boil 12 of the eggs for 4 minutes, rinse under cold water to stop the cooking. Cook the last egg 8 minutes, and reserve. Peel the eggs. Combine chaud-froid sauce with red food coloring, and coat 6 of the eggs and 3 of the asparagus tips with it. Dice and use the white and yolk of the hard boiled egg to create a design on each of the coated eggs. Mix the mayonnaise and cooked chicken, and divide it amongst the 6 tartlette shells. Place a glazed egg on top of each. Garnish the rest of the tartlette with the asparagus tips, one glazed, one unglazed. Fold the ham slices in quarters, arrange them in a circle, place an unglazed egg atop each slice, and garnish with a sliver of black olive.

239 calories per 2 egg serving.

Courtesy of
Jean-Paul Lacombe
Léon de Lyon
1, Rue Pléney
69001 Lyon FRANCE

Salads

Céleri en Remoulade
CELERY REMOULADE STYLE

Serves 4

    1/2 cup mayonnaise, fat-free
    1/2 cup sour cream, light
    1 tablespoon capers
    1 tablespoon fresh parsley -- chopped
    1 tablespoon gherkins -- finely chopped
    1 anchovy -- minced (optional)
    1 clove garlic -- minced
    1 tablespoon   dill -- chopped
    1 teaspoon lemon juice
    4 cups celery -- sliced very thin
    1 cup chicken stock

Combine all except celery and stock, cover and refrigerate several hours or overnight. Bring chicken stock to a boil in a saucepan, add celery, cover, and simmer until tender, about 8 minutes. Drain, mix with sauce. Refrigerate 2 hours or longer. Serve cold, arranging nicely on a few mixed greens.

75 calories per serving.

SALAD NIÇOISE

See picture in part I under Déjeuner. Note that in Nice, it's always canned tuna, and that the eggs are always quartered, not sliced.

Serves 4

    1 head Boston lettuce
    1 cup potatoes -- cooked, cold
    1 1/4 cups green beans -- cooked, 1" pieces
    1 can tuna in water -- about 6 oz.
    4 tomatoes -- quartered
    4 anchovy fillets
    1 small onion -- sliced
    12 black olives -- pitted
    2 eggs -- boiled 6 minutes
    4 tablespoons   olive oil
    2   tablespoons   vinegar
    1/4 teaspoon Dijon mustard

Page 100

Arrange the lettuce leaves among four salad dishes. Dice the potatoes, and toss with the beans. Arrange in a serving bowl. Drain the tuna, and add the tomatoes, the anchovies, the onion and the olives. Cut the eggs in quarters and add them. Place the vinegar in a small bowl, add salt, pepper, and mustard. Whisk in the oil. Spoon the vinaigrette over the salads, and serve.

288 calories per serving.

Une Salade de Base
A Basic Salad

Serves 4

1	whole	bibb lettuce -- or red leaf
5		asparagus spears -- blanched
1/2	cup	fresh peas -- blanched
1/2	cup	baby carrots -- blanched
1/2		sweet onions -- sliced thinly
1/2	large	tomato -- quartered
4	tablespoons	mustard vinaigrette -- see recipe

Combine all vegetables, cold, in a bowl. Add dressing and toss until well coated. Arrange on 4 salad plates.

109 calories per serving using the mustard vinaigrette under basic preparations, 41 calories without it.

Vegetables

Quiche des Brocolis
BROCCOLI QUICHE

Serves 4-6

4	pieces	phyllo pastry
15	ounces	chopped broccoli, frozen
1/4	cup	chicken stock
1	small	onion -- finely diced
2	cloves	garlic -- minced
3/4	cup	egg substitute
1/2	cup	nonfat sour cream
1	pinch	nutmeg
1	ounce	Swiss cheese -- grated

Preheat the oven to 350°F. Following directions carefully for keeping phyllo pastry moist while handling, spread one sheet of phyllo dough in the bottom of a 9" quiche pan (or pie plate) which has been sprayed with pan spray. Allow the sheet to overhang the edges for now. Spray the sheet with pan spray, then repeat with a second sheet at right angles to the first. Continue until all four sheet have been used. Fold over the excess phyllo dough, but don't fuss too much about how it looks. Spray the edges with pan spray to help them brown. If any of the sheets tear while placing them, it doesn't matter--just put them in and patch them up.

Prepare the broccoli according to the package directions, but only cook them halfway (the microwave is fine for this). Meanwhile, put the onion and garlic into a one quart saucepan and pour in the chicken broth. Bring to a boil, and allow to simmer five minutes until the onion is softened and the chicken broth is mostly gone. Put the broccoli and the onion-garlic mixture into the quiche pan on the phyllo pastry, and season with salt and pepper. Mix the egg substitute and the sour cream in a small mixing bowl with a whisk, and pour on top of the broccoli. Season with salt, pepper, and a pinch of nutmeg. Sprinkle with the cheese.

Bake for about 45 minutes until the center no longer jiggles when the quiche pan is agitated, and the top is golden brown. Allow to rest 10 minutes before serving.

172 calories for 1/4 of the quiche, as a vegetarian entree or lunch.
114 calories per 1/6 of quiche as a side dish.

Céleris-Branches Braisé
BRAISED CELERY

This recipe is for all of you who think of celery as a last resort diet food, stringy, and devoid of taste. Amazing what a little preparation can do to bring out the flavor in something!

Serves 4

1	bunch	celery
3	tablespoons butter, cut in small pieces	
1/2	cup white wine	
1/2	teaspoon	celery seed
1	teaspoon	herbs de Provence
1	tablespoon	cornstarch
2	tablespoons	parsley for garnish, fresh, minced

Trim the bunch of celery of leaves, and rinse well. Peel the stalks with a vegetable peeler to remove the strings, slice lengthwise in two and then again lengthwise in two, and cut diagonally into 2" lengths. Add butter, wine, celery seed, celery, and herbs to a medium sauté pan, and then add enough water to come up 2/3 of the way up the celery. Bring to a boil. Cover, reduce the heat to a simmer, and cook until the celery is tender but not mushy, perhaps 30 minutes. Remove the celery and keep hot. Simmer until the liquid is reduced to about 2 cups, make a slurry of the cornstarch with two tablespoons of cold water, and add it. Simmer and stir until the sauce thickens enough to coat the back of a wooden spoon. Sprinkle with parsley and serve. 99 calories per serving.

RATATOUILLE PROVENÇALE

This is a wonderful recipe for a vegetable that can be served hot, warm or cold. It's as at home on an elegant dinner plate as it is in a picnic basket. Enjoy!

Serves 4

2	large	onions
1	pound	tomatoes (or canned, see below)
1/2	pound	eggplant
2	cloves	garlic
2	teaspoons	oil
1	pound	zucchini, cut in julienne
2		green peppers, cut in julienne
1		bay leaf
2	branches	thyme (leaves only)
3	branches	parsley, chopped

Peel and slice the onions. Put the tomatoes in boiling water for one minute, and then run under cold water. Peel off the skins, halve, take out the seeds, then chop the tomatoes coarsely. You may also used an equivalent amount of canned peeled whole tomatoes, and chop them, draining off the juice. Peel the eggplant, and cut in large dice. Mince the garlic.

Heat the oil in a non-stick sauté pan, and brown the onions. When almost brown, add the garlic and sauté one minute. Add the tomatoes, eggplant, zucchini and green peppers, the bay leaf and the thyme, and salt and pepper to taste. Cover the pan tightly and cook on low for about an hour, more if the vegetables are not yet tender. Stir occasionally. If there is too much liquid, uncover the pan for a little while to let it evaporate. Remove the bay leaf. Season with salt and pepper. Serve warm or cold, garnishing with the chopped parsley.

91 calories per serving.

Gratin de Blettes a la Brebis du Lochois

GRATIN OF SWISS CHARD AND CHÈVRE

Recipe by Chef Jean Bardet--Château Belmont, Tours

Jean Bardet is a 54 year old native of Charente. He and his wife Sophie have two children, Valerie and Alice. In 1972, he finally found his dream house in Tours, a magnificent Napoleon III style mansion set in an English-style landscaped park of 7 1/2 acres. After fifteen years of preparation, the Chateau Belmont was opened as a hotel-restaurant, featuring fifteen four-star bedrooms in the hotel and eighty place settings in the

Château Belmont, Tours

restaurant. In 1985 he won his second Michelin star, and in 1991 he won four toques and a rating of 19 1/2 in Gault-Millau. He is a "Maître Cuisinier de France" since 1985.

"Cooking is the reflection of a life-standard, of a season, of a mood. Only the fresh seasonal products may be served. In France, we have forgotten that the most beautiful recipes come from poverty and not from luxury."--Jean Bardet

Jean Bardet also offers cooking courses every Thursday from 9AM to 3PM, after which he will serve you the 3 course lunch he has prepared along with selected wines and coffee.

Serves 4

2 1/4 pounds Swiss chard
1 tablespoon olive oil
1/2 lemon -- juice only
3 1/2 ounces chèvre cheese
6 1/2 ounces half and half
3 1/2 ounces heavy cream
2 egg yolks

Preheat the oven to 350°F. Remove the center filament from each large piece of chard, and cut them up into pieces of about 1" x 2". In a soup kettle with a cover, add one tablespoon of olive oil, the lemon juice, 1/2 cup of water, and bring to a boil. Add the Swiss chard, lower the heat, cover, and cook until tender. Stir occasionally.   Remove the cover, add the chèvre in small pieces, and boil away most of the water. Add the half and half, and bring to a boil. In a mixing bowl, stir the cream and the egg yolks, and season with salt and pepper. Take the pan with the chard off the heat, remove a 1/4 cup of the liquid and add it to the egg yolk mixture to warm it up, then add the egg yolk mixture back into the pan and mix thoroughly. Pour into a large pie pan or oven casserole, place in the oven and bake (uncovered) until golden, about 25 to 35 minutes. Serve the casserole at the table hot or warm.

313 calories serving four as a main dish, 156 calories serving 8 as a side dish.

Tarte aux Poireaux
LEEK TART

This is a simple but elegant recipe for a candlelight dinner for two, or for a dinner party, or even at room temperature at the beach—low in calories but high in satisfaction! It's truly one of my favorites. You could substitute onions if leeks are hard to find.

Serves 6

4	pieces	phyllo pastry
2		leeks
1/2	cup	chicken stock
1	clove	garlic -- minced
3/4	cup	egg substitute such as *Eggbeaters*®
1/2	cup	nonfat sour cream
2	ounces	Gruyère cheese (or Emmental or Swiss cheese)-- grated

Preheat oven to 350° F. Following directions carefully for keeping phyllo pastry moist while

handling, spread one sheet of phyllo dough in the bottom of a 9" tart pan or pie dish, preferably the removable bottom non-stick variety. Spray with pan spray, lay another sheet at right angles to the first, and continue until all four sheets are used. Allow edges to overhang for now. Cut the leeks where the green part just begins to lighten into the white, reserving the white and very light green parts for use here. Cut these in quarters lengthwise, then wash very well to remove the usual sand found in leeks. Dice, and simmer in the chicken stock until softened, 5 minutes or so, adding the garlic during the last minute. Drain and place in tart pan on the phyllo sheets. Whisk together egg substitute and sour cream in a mixing bowl until well mixed, season with salt and pepper, then pour over the leeks. Sprinkle with the cheese. Fold over excess phyllo dough at tart edges and spray with pan spray to help browning. Bake for about 45 minutes or until the center no longer jiggles when tart pan agitated, and top is golden brown. Allow to rest 5 to 10 minutes before serving.

120 calories per serving, 1/6 of tart.

Beef Dishes

Feuilles de Chou Farcies
STUFFED CABBAGE LEAVES

Serves 4

8	leaves	Savoy cabbage
6	ounces	ground beef
6	ounces	ground turkey
2	tablespoons	oil (divided)
1		onion -- chopped
2	ounces	mushrooms -- sliced thin
14	ounces	canned tomatoes -- whole (reserve juice)
3	ounces	ham slices, extra lean -- minced
1		egg
2	ounces	Gruyère cheese (or Swiss) grated
		nutmeg
2		apples, peeled -- cored, sliced thinly
1/2	cup	ketchup -- (yes, they do have and use ketchup! If you have the chance to

travel to France, try the *Amora* brand--it's terrific!)

1	tablespoon	mint leaves -- fresh, minced

Preheat the oven to 400°F. Wash the cabbage well and choose 8 nice large whole leaves. Put them in a pot and boil in water about 3 minutes until soft, immediately plunging them into ice water to stop the cooking. Mix the ground beef and turkey well in a mixing bowl.   Place one tablespoon of oil in a non-stick sauté pan, turn the heat to medium, and add the ground meat mixture, the onion and the mushrooms. Cook, stirring with a wooden spoon, about 5 minutes. Cut the tomatoes in half, scoop out the seeds, and add the tomatoes to the pot, reserving the juice. Add the ham, the egg, the cheese, a pinch of nutmeg, salt, pepper, and mix very well while cooking about 2 minutes.

Place a little of the stuffing in each cabbage leaf, and roll them up tucking in the edges so that the stuffing won't come out. Grease an ovenproof baking dish with the remaining oil, add the reserved tomato juice, the apple slices, the ketchup and the mint, mixing well. Then arrange the cabbage rolls on top. Cover with aluminum foil, and allow to bake about 45 minutes.

Remove the foil, and allow to bake a further 15 minutes. Serve 2 stuffed cabbages per person, and ladle a little of the sauce over each of them.

357 calories per person.

Paupiettes de Boeuf aux Aubergines

BRAISED BEEF PAUPIETTES WITH EGGPLANT

(Paupiettes are parcels or packets)

Recipe by Arnaud Poëtte, Chef de Cuisine, Hotel du Cap-Eden Roc

Drive down the long, winding driveway through the park-like setting of the exclusive Hotel Cap d'Antibes, and walk into the Eden-Roc dining room where you will look out at the Meditteranean Sea through a wall of glass. The exquisite table linens and settings of crystal and silver lend an elegant air to the setting. Meet chef Arnaud Poëtte, who has been here for 15 years, the last 6 of those as executive chef. He is an exacting individual, who runs his kitchen like a conductor directs an orchestra. The kitchen is large, and many cooks are preparing for the evening meal. The chef, however, takes the time and effort not only to prepare a recipe for us, but to cook the dish in front of us to show us how it's done. A tip--when you go-- try the lobster thermidor!

Serves 4

2 pounds eggplants
1 small bunch parsley,stems removed
14 ounces filet steaks
1 1/4 pounds tomatoes
1 lemon(zest & fruit)
12 leaves basil -- chopped

Entrance to the Eden Roc in Antibes

Peel and dice the eggplants, bake at 350°F for about 20 minutes or until tender. Purée the pulp in a blender, season with salt and pepper, and mix with some of the chopped parsley. Slice the filets into 12 slices and pound them flat. Spoon the purée onto the center of each, and roll them up, tying with kitchen string to form the paupiettes. Blanch the tomatoes in boiling water for a minute, so that the peel comes off easily. Cut them in quarters, squeeze lightly to remove the seeds, flatten the pulp and cut into dice (out of season you might prefer canned peeled tomatoes). Brown the paupiettes in a large non-stick pot, using pan spray. Add the diced tomato, stir, and cook gently for 30 minutes, stirring occasionally. Add the lemon zest and chopped basil leaves, season with salt and pepper. Remove the strings from the paupiettes. Spoon some of the sauce onto each pre-heated dinner plate, cut one of the paupiettes on a diagonal like a baguette and stand one side up, if desired, for presentation. Arrange a total of 3 paupiettes on each plate, and garnish with the remaining lemon and parsley.

Chef Arnaud Poëtte

279 calories per serving.

Ragoût de Boeuf

BEEF RAGOUT

Serves 2

1	teaspoon	butter
2	ounces	ham slices, extra lean -- cubed
1/2	pound	chuck roast -- cubed
2		carrots -- 2" slices
2	medium	onions -- chopped
2	medium	turnips -- peeled & chopped
2	cloves	garlic -- chopped
1	tablespoon	flour
1/4	cup	red wine
14	ounces	beef stock -- see recipe "Fonds Brun"
		bouquet garni
1	teaspoon	tomato purée
2	small	new potatoes
		rosemary sprigs for garnish

Heat the butter in a small soup kettle, and sauté the ham and beef pieces until seared on all sides. Remove the meat from the pot, turn the heat to medium-low, and slowly sauté the carrots, onions, turnips and garlic. Return the beef and ham to the pot, sprinkle with the flour, and mix well. Continue cooking and stirring the mixture a few minutes to dispel the floury taste, then add the wine and just enough broth to cover the meat and vegetables. Add the bouquet garni, tomato purée, and salt and pepper.

Cover and bring to a slow simmer, cooking about 1 1/2 to 2 hours. Peek in occasionally and stir, adding a little more beef stock if the sauce reduces too quickly. Meanwhile, in a small saucepan, boil the new potatoes until soft, and add to the kettle 10 minutes before serving. Ladle the hot ragoût into serving bowls, and garnish with the sprigs of rosemary.

452 calories.

Chateaubriand à la Béarnaise
FILET MIGNON WITH BÉARNAISE SAUCE

Can you really believe I'm going to suggest that you can eat this famous, hearty beef dish on a diet? You bet I am! And just wait till you tuck into a thick piece of this succulent cut, roasted and smothered in Béarnaise sauce--it's heaven! For an alternate and slightly more modern interpretation, slice the tenderloin into four one-inch thick steaks, salt and pepper both sides, grill to medium rare on a charcoal or gas grill, and serve with the sauce.

Serves 4
1 to 1 1/2* pounds beef tenderloin--the best you can find!
2 cloves garlic, peeled, halved (optional)
1 cup Béarnaise sauce (see recipe)
      flat parsley, chopped, for garnish

Prepare the Béarnaise sauce first, and keep it warm in a vacuum bottle. Fire up a charcoal grill, and let the flames die down so that the coals have just turned gray, or preheat a gas grill to high. Dry the roast well, and salt and pepper both sides. You may, if you wish, rub the outside of the meat with the garlic. Place the meat on the grill, and sear all six sides. Then cover the roast with the grill cover, or a cover fashioned from aluminum foil, and set away from the center of the heat (simply turn a gas grill down to medium-low). Check the internal temperature of the meat with an instant reading thermometer, and cook to your desired doneness: 120°F for very rare, 140°F for medium, and...that's as far as I'll recommend you cook it (if you get to 160°F it will be well done but also gray and tasteless). Remove the roast from the fire, cover with aluminum foil and then a kitchen towel, and *allow to rest*. This is a very important step, because if you cut into the meat immediately, the juices will not have time to reabsorb into the meat. After ten minutes, remove the cover and slice into four steaks. Center each on a preheated dinner plate, and ladle a quarter cup of Béarnaise sauce in front of the steak. Garnish with the chopped parsley.

    *At 1 pound, that's 401 calories. At 1 1/4 pounds it's 480 calories, and at 1 1/2 pounds it's 560 calories with the sauce.   If you choose low-fat beef like *Maverick Ranch Natural Lite®*, you'll save about 62 % on the beef, dropping the calorie count e.g. for *1 1/2 lb. to 263 calories!*

TOURNEDOS CHASSEUR

Serves 4
| 20 | ounces | beef tenderloin ends -- or Filet Mignon |
| 1 | cup | Sauce Chasseur -- see recipe |

This, although a classic French dish, is more of an idea as to what to do with the sauce than a recipe. Go ahead and try it though, you'll be pleasantly surprised.

Carefully cut the tenderloin up into one inch thick slices, so that if you are really using the small ends at the end of the tenderloin you will have about 12 pieces. These are called "tournedos" of beef, and may be tied with string to keep their round shape if desired. If you are using filet mignon, you may cut it up as above, or just slice it into four steaks.

Grill the beef on a charcoal or gas grill to your desired doneness, and serve with the Sauce Chasseur.

448 calories each serving.

Variation:
TOURNEDOS BRABANÇONNE

Try this with steamed spinach. It goes well with the steak, is low in calories, and is easy to prepare!

One recipe tartlettes four 4, prepared without the sugar (see basics)
One recipe Mornay Sauce (see Sauce Béchamel)
2 packages frozen Brussels sprouts, boiled according to package directions
20 ounces beef tenderloin tips, grilled

Prepare 4 phyllo tartlets following the recipe but omitting the sugar, and fill them with boiled Brussels sprouts. Top with Sauce Mornay, then top with three grilled tournedos of beef as described above.

498 calories per serving.

Veal

Blanquette de Veau
WHITE RAGOÛT OF VEAL

This stew is from the peasant kitchens of the Languedoc. A blanquette, in general, is a white ragoût, usually of lamb, chicken or fish, bound with a liaison of eggs and cream, and accompanied by pearl onions and mushrooms. It is a very classic French dish, which here has been lightened in calories and which still retains a great deal of its original integrity and flavor. Since the stew has a nice sauce, consider serving with rice or noodles--a quick look at the calorie count and you can see with this recipe you can afford it!

Serves 6

2	pounds	veal cubes -- about 1" each
2		carrots -- rough cut
2		leeks -- washed and quartered
1		onion -- stuck with 3 cloves
5	cloves	garlic
		bouquet garni
1/2	pound	mushroom caps
1/2	pound	pearl onions -- peeled
4	teaspoons	flour
2	teaspoons	butter -- at room temperature
1/3	cup	half and half
1/4	teaspoon	nutmeg
		flat parsley for garnish

Place the veal in a soup kettle, cover with water, and bring to a boil. Discard the water, and again cover with water, and bring to a boil. Skim, then add the carrots, leeks, onion with cloves, garlic and bouquet garni. Cover and simmer about one hour. Meanwhile, put the pearl onions and mushrooms in a small saucepan, cover with water and boil about 5 minutes. Drain and reserve. Remove the garlic and veal from the soup kettle and reserve. Then remove the remaining flavoring ingredients and discard them. Mash the butter with the flour into a paste to make a beurre manié. Bring the veal stock to a boil and reduce to about 2 cups. If there is too little liquid, add water to make 2 cups and bring to a boil. Add the beurre manié, and cook a few minutes to thicken the sauce, add the half and half, then add the reserved veal and garlic, the mushrooms and the onions. Season with salt, pepper, and nutmeg. Serve, garnishing with the parsley.

248 calories.

Osso-Bucco à la Biére
VEAL SHANKS BRAISED IN BEER

As best I can tell, this is a Milanese dish that was re-interpreted in the north of France. Many Italian dishes are found regularly prepared in all parts of France, and one sees a great deal of pasta in the south, but finding this dish on the North coast was a very pleasant surprise to me! Here's my reinterpretation for us:

Serves 4

4	veal shanks	8 ounces each, trimmed of all visible fat
4	ounces dark beer	
2	carrots peeled & sliced	
15	ounces whole canned tomatoes, quartered	
1	stalk celery	
2	small onions	
1	bay leaf	
1	teaspoon rosemary	
1	teaspoon thyme	
1	teaspoon parsley	
1	lemon, juice only	

In a non-stick sauté pan sprayed with pan spray, place the veal shanks over low heat and brown on all sides. Meanwhile, add 8 ounces of water to a soup kettle, and add the next nine ingredients (beer through parsley), bring to a boil, then simmer ten minutes. Add the browned veal. The liquid should come halfway up the sides of the veal--add more water if necessary. Cover and let simmer about two hours, turning the shanks over about halfway through the cooking. Remove the bay leaf. If the soup exceeds two cups, reduce it. Place each veal shank in the center of a pre-heated soup plate, ladle the sauce over and around the veal, and sprinkle with the lemon juice. Season with salt and pepper. Serve hot.

337 calories per serving.

Pork Entrees

Carré de Porc Normande
NORMANDY-STYLE PORK TENDERLOINS

Normandy is one of the great cooking centers of France. It is home to a large cattle and dairy industry, and perhaps because of the availability of cream, butter, and beef, its cuisine tends to be heavier than elsewhere in France--and so do its people (beware)! Also extremely important to the cooking of this region are apples and apple brandy (Calvados), which are used in all kinds of dishes.

Serves 6

     2 pounds pork tenderloin
     1/2 teaspoon ground cumin
     1 tablespoon butter
     2 tablespoons   Calvados -- (Apple Brandy)
     1/2 cup half and half
     1/4 cup milk
     1 tablespoon cornstarch
                    chopped parsley for garnish

Slice the pork tenderloins on a diagonal about 3/4 inch thick to make medallions. Season with salt and pepper, then with the cumin. Melt the butter in a non-stick skillet over low heat. Add the pork medallions, and cook slowly until just cooked through (do not overcook or the medallions will be tough). Remove the pork from the skillet, and keep warm, covering with foil.

Add the Calvados to the skillet, and with a wooden spoon scrape up any bits at the bottom. Bring to a boil and add the half and half. Stir the cornstarch into the cold milk, and add to the sauce, and bring to a simmer while stirring to thicken the sauce. Adjust the seasonings with salt and pepper, if necessary. Put the pork medallions back in the skillet just long enough to warm them up, and then fan them out on a pre-heated serving plate, spooning the sauce over them. Garnish with the chopped parsley.

Try preparing some rice for a side dish, but instead of just spooning it onto the plate, pack it into a mold first, then invert it on the plate. If you don't have a timbale mold, a ramekin or coffee cup will do. Spray the mold with pan spray for easy removal. Put a sliver of black truffle (or black olive—poor man's truffles), a sprig of parsley, or a diamond shaped piece of red pepper on top!

253 calories (without the rice).

Côtes de Porc Grillées à L'Ardennaise
GRILLED PORK CHOPS, ARDENNAISE STYLE

The Ardennes is a thick forest with fine hunting, and pigs and wild boar are found in abundance. It is on the Belgian border in the flatlands of northeastern France, where some hearty eating can be found. This recipe, slightly adapted from the classical one, is likewise hearty eating--but at an affordable calorie count!

Serves 6

24		pearl onions*
6	medium	potatoes, peeled
6	lean pork chops	(about 3 pounds)
4	slices	bacon
1	tablespoon	butter
1	tablespoon	sugar
	sprigs of thyme for garnish	

*Note: If pearl onions are not available, prepare chopped onions sautéed in butter, and omit the sugar.

Prepare a charcoal fire or preheat a gas grill. Cut an X in the bottom of the pearl onions, just through the skin. Boil in a small saucepan one minute. Drain them, and peel. Place them back in the saucepan in boiling water. Boil 12 minutes. Slice the potatoes and boil them in a separate saucepan about 5 to 7 minutes until just beginning to soften--don't cook them all the way. Drain all the vegetables, and rinse them in cold water to stop the cooking. Set aside. Over a hot charcoal fire or on a gas grill, grill the pork chops until just cooked through (if you overcook them they will be tough). When done, set them aside but keep warm. While the chops are grilling, dice the bacon, put it in a non-stick skillet, and cook until fat begins to render. Sauté the partially cooked potatoes in the bacon fat on low heat, until tender. Melt the tablespoon of butter in a non-stick skillet over low heat, add the onions, and heat through. Add the tablespoon of sugar to the onions, and stir to caramelize.

To serve, place one pork chop on a pre-heated dinner plate. Surround with fried potatoes, diced bacon, and glazed onions. Garnish with the sprigs of thyme.

355 calories.

Porc Farci aux Pruneaux et aux Pommes-Fruits
ROAST LOIN OF PORK WITH PRUNES AND APPLES

This is an adaptation of a dish I ate in Tours, which is in the heartland of France south of Paris. Tours is well known for its many chateaux (the Loire Valley), and as home to artists and writers. This is also a country renown for its roasts, which are all the more wonderful for their simplicity. The skill of roasting in the Touraine becomes more important when one realizes that there are few seasonings or sauces used in this region. This recipe is my version of a favorite regional dish from this region.

Serves 6

1/2 cup prunes -- pitted
1 1/2 cups port wine
1 1/2 pounds pork tenderloin -- trim all fat
1 1/2 teaspoons oil
2 pounds apples -- peeled & cored

1 cup chicken broth
1/2 cup apple cider
1/4 cup half and half
2 teaspoons cornstarch

Preheat the oven to 325°F. Place the prunes and the port wine in a saucepan and bring to a simmer for about 15 minutes. Meanwhile, make a slit down one side of the pork most but not all the way through. If using more than one pork tenderloin to make up the 1 1/2 pounds, do this with each tenderloin. Flatten the pork slightly, using a mallet if necessary.   Drain the prunes, reserve the port, and place the prunes in the center of the pork. Roll the pork roast together and tie with kitchen string. Heat the oil in a skillet and brown the pork roast on all sides. Don't wash the skillet. Place the roast on a rack coated with cooking spray, and the rack in a shallow roasting pan. Slide the roast into the oven, and bake about one and a quarter hours, or until a meat thermometer slid into the meat reads 155°F. The pork should be slightly pink--don't overcook it or it will be dry! Remove the roast, and let stand, covered, in a warm place for 10 minutes.

Meanwhile, quarter the apples, and boil them in a saucepan 10 to 15 minutes or *just until soft*. Do not overcook or you will have applesauce! Reserve the apples. Place the roasting pan on the stove on medium heat, pour in the port and with a wooden spoon scrape up the brown bits in the bottom of the pan. When simmering, pour the port and pan juices into the skillet, set on high heat. Add the chicken stock and the apple cider, and boil until reduced to about 1 3/4 cups, which may take five minutes or less. Whisk together the cold half and half and the cornstarch, and add it to the skillet, stirring for one minute to thicken the sauce. Strain the sauce back into the saucepan, add the apples and heat through. Season with salt and pepper. Slice the roast on the diagonal in 3/4 inch slices, and lay them out overlapping on pre-heated dinner plates. Spoon some of the apple-port wine cream sauce on and around the roast, and serve.

378 calories.

Rabbit

Rabbit is found commonly on French tables, like chicken is here.   Explore your local supermarket and you may find rabbit available in the frozen meat section.   It is tasty, and very low in calories and fat.   Here is a chance to get acquainted, all within your diet.

Monsieur le boucher *shows how to properly cut up a rabbit, in Paris*

Lapin Normand
RABBIT NORMANDY STYLE

Serves 6
  1 rabbit, cut in serving portions (see picture--but you needn't be so exact)
          flour for dredging
  3 small onions-- chopped roughly
  2 bottles hard apple cider (usually in the beer section)
  1 tablespoon   oil
  2 carrots -- chopped roughly
  6 new potatoes
  2 tablespoons chopped parsley
  1 tablespoon   cornstarch
  3 apples -- peeled,cored,sliced
       parsley for garnish

Dredge the rabbit pieces in the flour. Heat the oil in a soup kettle. Add the pieces of rabbit and the onion and brown in the oil, turning as needed, for about 20 minutes on a low flame. Add the cider, turning the fire up momentarily. Using a wooden spoon, scrape up the brown bits at the bottom of the pot. When the cider boils, add the potatoes and the carrots. Turn down the fire to a simmer, cover and cook one-half hour. Remove the cover, add the apples, and cook another half-hour. At this point, boil rapidly until the liquid in the pot is about 2 cups. Make a slurry of two tablespoons of cold water and the cornstarch, and add it and the parsley, cooking until the sauce is thick enough to coat a spoon. Plate the rabbit and vegetables and spoon the sauce over them. Garnish with the sprigs of parsley.

252 calories.

Lapin à la Moutarde
RABBIT IN MUSTARD SAUCE

Serves 4

1	rabbit
1/2	cup Dijon mustard
1	tablespoon butter
1	tablespoon oil
1/4	cup brandy
1 1/2	tablespoons flour
2	medium onions -- chopped
1	quart chicken stock
1/8	teaspoon ground cloves
1	bay leaf
1	teaspoon thyme -- minced
1	teaspoon rosemary -- minced
1	tablespoon parsley -- minced

If whole, cut the rabbit up into serving pieces. Put the mustard in a mixing bowl, add the rabbit and mix thoroughly to coat. Don't wash out the bowl. Melt the butter and add the oil to a large soup kettle. Place the rabbit in the kettle over medium heat and brown, on all sides. Remove the rabbit and place back in the mixing bowl. Add the brandy, turn the heat up, and boil until the brandy is almost gone. Lower the heat to medium, add the onions, and stir, cooking for 2 minutes. Sprinkle the flour over the rabbit, stir and cook one more minute. Add a little of the stock, and stir with a wooden spoon to dissolve the brown bits at the bottom of the pan. Add the remaining stock, the reserved rabbit, the cloves, bay leaf, thyme, rosemary, parsley, and any remaining mustard from the mixing bowl. Season with salt and pepper. Bring to a simmer, and cook uncovered about 1 1/2 hours, turning the meat as it becomes exposed. Remove the bay leaf. Reduce the sauce until thick. Serve hot, ladling the sauce over and around the rabbit.

Great served over boiled rice!   429 calories.

Poultry
CASSOULET

Cassoulet always was the essence of peasant fare. It is one of those farmhouse dishes that started out in a big pot on the back of the stove, never emptied, never allowed to grow cold, always refilled

with whatever was at hand. However, with the passage of time it has become more and more celebrated as the outstanding dish of the Languedoc region. Three cities today all claim to have the recipe for the *true* Cassoulet, all varying in exactly what's to be put in the pot. The features in common are the beans, the goose fat, the onion, the cloves, and the garlic, but Castelnaudary, Toulouse and Carcassone are fiery rivals when it comes to the rest of the ingredients. Can this dish, which in any of its original forms contains a whopping 1200 to 1400 calories per portion, be transformed into something one can eat which is not as laden with calories as it is with goose fat? Is it possible to have retained any of the feeling of the original dish? This version below is a very credible adaptation of Cassoulet, while containing only a third of the calories!

Serves 8

1/2   pound turkey sausage
1/2   pound duck meat without skin (use the legs and save the duck breasts for Magret de Canard--see recipe)
1/2   pound pork tenderloin -- lean, boneless,cubed
1/2   pound lamb, cubed -- lean
1   large onion -- sliced
5   cloves garlic -- minced
2   tablespoons flour
1/2   cup dry white wine
1   cup chicken stock
2   tablespoons parsley
1   bay leaf
1   dash ground cloves
1   whole carrot
1   rib celery
15   ounces tomatoes, canned -- diced
2   cans cannelini beans
3/4   cup bread crumbs

Cassoulet as served in Toulouse

Spray a flameproof casserole with cooking spray, and on medium-high heat, cook the sausages and the duck legs until browned on all sides. Remove both to a plate, and add the pork and lamb. Brown on all sides, then add the onion and cook till onion is tender. Add the garlic, sauté two more minutes. Sprinkle the flour over the mixture, and mix well. Add the white wine and chicken stock. Put the duck legs and sausages back in the pot, and bring to a boil. With a wooden spoon, stir, scraping up the brown bits at the bottom. Add the parsley, bay leaf, cloves, carrot, celery, and tomatoes in their sauce.

At the "Factory Store" of La Belle Chaurienne in Castelnaudary, discussing the merits of their Cassoulet

Bring to a boil, the lower the heat to a simmer. Allow to cook, uncovered, one hour.

Preheat the oven to 325°F. Remove the bay leaf, the carrot, the celery and the duck from the kettle. Remove the meat from the duck bones, add the meat back into the casserole, and stir in the beans, with their liquid.

In the walled city of Carcassone...

Bake 45 minutes as follows. After the first fifteen minutes, open the oven and sprinkle 1/4 cup of the breadcrumbs on top. After the next 15 minutes, stir the crumbs into the cassoulet and again spread 1/4 cup of the breadcrumbs on the top. After the final 15 minutes, stir the crumbs into the cassoulet, sprinkle the last 1/4 cup bread crumbs on top, spray them with pan spray, and broil until golden brown. Serve right from the casserole, or ladle into individual pre-heated earthenware bowls.

...no shortage of Cassoulet!

402 calories per serving.

Page 120

QUAIL

Chef Henri Patey of the Culinary Institute of America at Greystone in the Napa Valley taught me how to bone a quail. Actually, it's no different than boning a chicken—only a lot more tedious since the quail is a lot smaller. If you can find quail that are not boneless, you can bone them yourself, leaving the drumsticks in, without much difficulty. Remove the wings. Push the drumsticks up and separate the joint. Bone out the shoulder blade on one side, then the ribs, being very careful not to cut through to or tear the skin. Then do the other side, meeting in the middle, and remove the bones. Even if you end up with a hole or two, the recipe will still work.

Cailles aux Crabes
CRABMEAT STUFFED QUAIL

Serves 4

1	teaspoon	butter
4	tablespoons	onion -- minced
1/4	cup	egg substitute such as *Eggbeaters*®
1	tablespoon	herbs de Provence
2	tablespoons	mayonnaise-- lowfat
6	ounces	crabmeat -- jumbo lump, drained
2	tablespoons	bread crumbs (maximum)
1/4	teaspoon	dry mustard
4	tablespoons	celery -- minced
4		quail -- semi-boneless
1/4		teaspoon paprika

1/2 recipe for Sauce Aurore (see under Sauce Béchamel)

Preheat the oven to 400°F. Place butter in a small sauté pan, and sauté the onion. Remove from the pan, and place in a mixing bowl. Beat in the egg substitute, then add the herbs, the lowfat mayo, and fold in the crabmeat without breaking up the lumps. Next, add as little of the breadcrumbs as you can. The amount of breadcrumbs you need depends on the water content of the crabmeat, and is used to absorb the liquid so it won't drain out. Add the mustard and celery and mix carefully. Chill at least 30 minutes. Meanwhile, open up the quail and dry, inside and out. Take a sheet of aluminum foil and fold a rectangle about the size of the quail, folding up the sides to make a shoe-box-shaped "boat". Spray the boats with vegetable oil spray. Stuff each of the quail with about 1/4 cup of the chilled mixture, wrapping the skin well around and forming into a quail-shaped package. Dust with paprika. Secure with two toothpicks each to hold the quail together. Place in the aluminum foil boats, toothpick side down. Spray the outside of the quail with vegetable oil spray. Place the boats on a cookie sheet in the oven and roast about 25-30 minutes, until golden brown. Place the quail on the plate, spoon the sauce over the quail, garnish with a little parsley and serve immediately.

349 calories per serving, with 1/4 cup sauce per person.

CHICKEN

Coq Au Vin
CHICKEN IN RED WINE

Actually "rooster in wine", but roosters are hard to find, and tend to be so tough they require a long cooking time. Most French housewives are using the more tender chicken these days. The dish has its roots in the Touraine, that wonderful stretch of French heartland just southwest of Paris, well-known for the chateaux (castles) of the Loire Valley. I think the dish began life as "Coq au Chambertin", but few can afford to *drink* such expensive burgundy nowadays--much less cook with it. Therefore, I suggest you use an inexpensive but palatable red table wine. *Don't cook with anything you wouldn't drink!*

Serves 4

4   slices bacon
2   pounds chicken parts without skin, defatted -- bone-in
      flour for dredging
1/3   cup onion -- finely chopped
4   cloves garlic -- minced
1/4   cup brandy -- warm
1 1/4 cups red wine
1/2   teaspoon thyme -- dried
1 1/2 cups chicken stock
2   teaspoons tomato paste
12   small onions -- about 1" diameter
1   tablespoon sugar
1/2   pound mushrooms
1   teaspoon cornstarch (about)

Cut the bacon into lardons, about 1/4" across and 1" long. Place them in a large casserole over medium heat, fry until fat is rendered and bacon is browned, then remove them and reserve. Dredge the chicken parts in the flour. Sauté the chicken parts in the bacon fat until lightly browned on all sides. Then remove the chicken and reserve. Add the chopped onion, sauté for about three minutes. Add the minced garlic, sauté about one additional minute. Turn the heat up to high. Add most of the brandy, reserving a ladleful. Keeping yourself well away from the pot, ignite the brandy in the ladle with a match, and add it to the pot. When the flames have subsided, stir with a wooden spoon to dissolve the brown bits on the bottom of the pan. Boil until almost gone. Add a little of the red wine, stir again if any brown bits remain, then add the thyme, the chicken stock and tomato paste, and stir well. Add the chicken, and if not completely covered, add water to cover. Simmer about 25 minutes, until tender.

While the chicken is cooking, prepare the onions as follows. Cut an X just through the skin of each onion, at the bottom. In a medium non-stick sauté pan, place the onions and enough water to cover. Bring to a boil, and the simmer about one minute. Drain, rinse with cold water, then peel the onions. Place the onions back in the sauté pan with two tablespoons of water and one tablespoon of sugar. Cook over medium heat, stirring, until onions are caramelized nicely. Reserve.

Remove the chicken from the pot, add the mushrooms to the sauce, and simmer 5 minutes or until soft. Then, boiling rapidly, reduce the sauce to about 2 cups. Reduce the heat. Make a slurry of the cornstarch with 2 tablespoons of cold water and add to the sauce, stirring to thicken. Adjust the amount of cornstarch as needed to achieve a reasonably thick consistency. Add the reserved onions, the bacon, the chicken, and season with salt and pepper. Simmer about 5 minutes (do not boil), until heated through. Serve immediately.

467 calories

Poularde Mijotée sur un Lit de Legumes du Soleil
CHICKEN SIMMERED ON A BED OF MEDITTERANEAN VEGETABLES

Recipe by Chef Christian Willer, The Hotel Martinez, Cannes

You are standing on the Croisette, the world famous boulevard in Cannes that looks out on the

The Bay of Cannes from the Hotel Martinez

beaches of the Meditteranean Sea on one side, and glittering hotels, elegant shops and cafes on the other. The Martinez, an art-deco styled hotel now just completely renovated, cuts a handsome figure in the skyline of Cannes. The hotel has been host to numerous heads of state, and is the choice of such guests as Paul Valery, Duke of Montmorency, André Citroën, and more recently, Peter Ustinov, Christopher Reeve, Charleston Heston, Jacques Chirac and on and on....

The hotel's restaurant, La Palme d'Or, was created in 1985, and named for the most prestigious award given by the famed international film festival held annually in May in Cannes. As part of its commitment to quality, the hotel chose a famous chef, Christian Willer, native of Alsace, to head the kitchen. He has trained at Maxim's and Prunier in Paris, as well as at numerous other well known restaurants in France. He holds two coveted Michelin stars for his excellence, and with his ability to revive the flavors of Provence in each one of his dishes, puts to shame the would-be Provençal cooking all the rage at the moment.

Chef Christian Willer

Try his sea-perch with a caviar potato crust, or his Sisteron lamb roasted with parsley and green garlic. A heady experience is yours with any choice from amongst his selections. Here, he has been kind enough to create a recipe just for us that I think you will agree is divine.

Serves 4

1	pound	cremini mushrooms -- (cépes)
1	bunch	Italian parsley -- (flat leaf)
4		chicken breasts without skin
4	sprigs	rosemary -- fresh
1	small	fennel bulb -- diced
8		artichoke hearts
4		plum tomatoes
1	medium	onion
1 1/2	ounces	olive oil
4	cloves	garlic
2		baby leeks -- or scallions
5	tablespoons	black olives -- diced
1	tablespoon	balsamic vinegar
		sea salt, freshly ground pepper

Preheat the oven to 425°F. Clean the mushrooms, if necessary. Separate the heads from the stems, and finely dice the stems, reserving the heads. Simmer the chopped mushrooms in a non-stick pan using cooking spray, and cook until the juice they release is evaporated completely. Season them with salt and pepper, and allow to cool. Add one tablespoon of chopped parsley.

Make slits lengthwise in the chicken breasts and stuff them with the mushroom-parsley mixture. Separate the stalks of the rosemary from the leaves, reserving the leaves. Cut the stalks into two or three pieces, and use them to join the edges of the chicken and skewer them closed. Dice the fennel, halve the artichoke hearts if large, halve the tomatoes, peel the onion and slice it thinly, wash and slice the leeks. Warm the olive oil in the bottom of an ovenproof casserole, and add the vegetables. Add the garlic cloves and the mushroom heads. Cook until vegetables are translucent.

Now, place the chicken breasts on top of the vegetables. Add 1/2 cup of water, place a tight-fitting cover on top and bake 15 minutes. Remove the chicken, and add the remaining parsley, diced olives, and balsamic vinegar, mixing gently. Divide the vegetables among four pre-heated dinner plates, place the chicken breasts on top removing the rosemary twigs. Drizzle a little of the cooking juice on each chicken breast to moisten. Garnish with the rosemary leaves, and serve hot. [Note: If fennel is unavailable, try replacing it with celery and some fennel seed.]

430 calories.

Poulet au Cidre
CHICKEN IN CIDER

This is a classical dish of Normandy, that northeastern section of France along the seacoast just east of Brittany. Normandy is a large province, but it is particularly well known for the famous Mont-Saint-Michel. The Mont is surrounded by sand, which slopes in a

Mont-Saint-Michel from the causeway

barely discernible way for ten miles out to sea. At low tide, the Mont is surrounded by quicksand. The tide will rise forty-five feet or more as it comes in, covering more than ten miles. The tide comes in so fast that it is said to have overtaken a running horse, and at high tide therefore, the Mont is an island, connected to the mainland only by a recently built causeway. Don't park in certain areas of the parking lot at the foot of Mont-Saint-Michel or your car will be overtaken by the sea!

Cider and Calvados (apple brandy) are used in many dishes in Normandy, where in other regions of France white wine would be used. Also note the use of butter, for which this area is renown, rather than olive oil as would be used in the South. I ate *Poulet au Cidre* in a little restaurant high up in the tiny medieval city that is Mont-Saint-Michel, and it is a wonderful reminder of all that this area is known for, incorporating apples, apple cider and Calvados in a satisfying and tasty dish.

Serves 4

1/2 cup raisins
1/3 cup Calvados
1 tablespoon butter
2 pounds chicken parts without skin, defatted -- bone-in
2 onions -- thinly sliced
1 clove garlic -- finely chopped
12 ounces apple cider
1 bouquet garni (parsley, thyme and a bay leaf tied in cheesecloth)
1 apple peeled & cored
1 tablespoon cornstarch

The sign warns plainly about the incoming tide...

...but not everyone listens!

Place the raisins in a small bowl with the Calvados and allow to steep. Melt the butter in a soup kettle, and sauté the chicken on all sides until brown. Remove the chicken, set aside, and add the onions to the pot. Cook these on low heat until they begin to color, about 25 minutes. Raise the heat to medium, and add the garlic. Sauté one minute. Pour the Calvados into the pot, leaving the raisins behind momentarily. Turn up the heat, and boil rapidly until almost gone, stirring to incorporate any brown bits on the bottom of the pan. Add the cider, the raisins, the bouquet garni, and the reserved chicken, cover and simmer about 15 minutes.

Cut the apple up into chunks. Add them to the kettle and simmer about 20 more minutes, until chicken and apple are both tender. Remove the bouquet garni. Add water or reduce sauce as necessary, so that there is about 1 cup. Make a slurry with 2 tablespoons of cold water and the cornstarch, and add it to the kettle, stirring until the sauce thickens. Serve family style.

398 calories per serving.

Poulet Aux Amandes
CHICKEN IN ALMOND SAUCE

Don't be put off by the list of ingredients--this one is simple but tasty!

Serves 4

2	pounds	chicken parts without skin, defatted -- bone-in
1	bunch	fresh thyme leaves
1	teaspoon	oil
2	cups	white wine
2		bay leaves
1		clove
2		eggs -- hard-boiled
3 1/2	ounces	almonds
3	cloves	garlic
6	ounces	skim milk
1	pinch	saffron
1	tablespoon	butter
1	tablespoon	flour

Season the pieces of chicken with thyme, salt and pepper, and brown in a non-stick pan using the oil. Pour off any excess oil, add the wine, the bay leaves and the clove. Cover and cook 25 minutes on a low heat.

In a blender or food processor, pulse the eggs, the almonds and the garlic until chopped fine, then add the milk and saffron. Remove the chicken and keep it warm, then add the almond mixture to the pan. Knead the butter and flour together to form a paste called a beurre manié. You will only use about two teaspoons of it, but it is too hard to knead such a small quantity. Bring the almond mixture to a boil, then add the beurre manié in small bits until the sauce is nicely thickened. Adjust the seasoning, plate the chicken and spoon on the sauce. Garnish with some sprigs of fresh thyme.

424 calories.

Poulet Roti aux Pamplemousses et au Poivre Rose
ROASTED CHICKEN WITH GRAPEFRUIT AND PINK PEPPERCORNS

Recipe by Michel Guérard of Les Prés d'Eugénie

We wish to thank M. Guérard for his interest in this book and his wonderful contribution. Les

Prés d'Eugénie is a chateau in the southwest of France, at Eugénie-les Bains. From the moment you enter, you sense that this is home for the Guérards, Michel and Christine. This is country elegance at its finest, with its "modest" nineteenth century decor. The chef is perhaps best known for his invention of Cuisine Minceur in the nineteen seventies, a fresh new look at French cooking that emphasized fresh vegetables and techniques to enhance rather than smother the flavors of the food. His ideas created a movement in France that resulted

Les Prés d'Eugénie, Eugénie-les-Bains, France

in the lightening of many traditional dishes into the dishes we see served today. He is today still considered one of the foremost chefs of France, and has the distinction of three stars from Michelin, and a 19.5 out of 20 from Gault-Millau (highest honors). Today, he serves both a menu minceur and a menu gourmand. While the menu changes from time to time, some specialties we like include an aspic of grilled langoustines on salad with crispy galettes, and wild rabbit and duckling pie with foie gras. To finish, try the three sorbets: grapes, rhubarb, and red fruits, with garden verbena ice cream. In the words of Gault-Millau, "unqualified bliss!"

Serves 4

1 chicken	1 stalk celery
1 tablespoon olive oil	1 bouquet garni(bay leaf, parsley, and thyme tied in cheesecloth)
3 pink grapefruits	1 ounce veal demi-glace*
3 white grapefruits	1 tablespoon cornstarch
1 carrot	2 tablespoons pink peppercorns
1 onion	

* You can use a prepared veal demi-glaze such as Demi-Glace Gold, sold in fine supermarkets and gourmet shops, or make your own. If veal is unavailable, you can make a brown stock (see fonds brun), and reduce it until it becomes very rich and thick. If you try this with canned chicken stock the result will be decidedly inferior, but at least be sure you buy low-salt stock. Otherwise when you reduce it, it will be much too salty.

Preparation and Cooking of the Chicken:

Have the butcher remove the innards and prepare the chicken. Preheat the oven to 400°F. Brush the chicken with olive oil, salt it and pepper it outside and inside. Put it in a casserole, and bake, uncovered, about one hour while basting it regularly.

Preparation of the Garnish:

Using a sharp knife, peel one pink grapefruit and one white grapefruit. Then, pass the knife blade between the membranes, detach the segments and reserve them. Juice the other grapefruits, and reserve the juice. Peel and wash the carrot, the onion, the celery, slice them thinly. Add them to the pot around the chicken along with the bouquet garni as soon as the one hour of initial cooking time is up, then continue to bake an additional 30 minutes. Five to six minutes before the end of cooking, pour the demi-glace and the juice of the grapefruits over the vegetables.

With a spatula turn and mix the con-tents of the pan well, as well as scraping the bottom to add the brown bits to the sauce. Take the chicken out of the dish, drain it well, put it on a dish to rest and keep warm on the door of the oven.

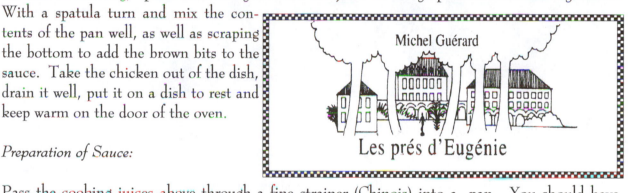

Preparation of Sauce:

Pass the cooking juices above through a fine strainer (Chinois) into a pan. You should have about one to one and one-half cups. If there is more, reduce it by boiling on a high heat; if too little, add a little demi-glaze and grapefruit juice. Place it back on the stove and add the cornstarch diluted in 1 tablespoon of cold water, and add the pink peppercorns. Stirring, simmer the sauce about 2 minutes. Don't let it boil. Lower the fire to medium, and add the reserved grapefruit sections.

Finish and Presentation:

Cut up the chicken and remove the skin. Arrange the chicken pieces on a hot platter, spoon some sauce over the chicken, and decorate it with the grapefruit sections coated with a little sauce.

This dish would be accompanied nicely by seasonal vegetables.

316 calories.

Volaille Marinée, Celeri et Oseille Crue
MARINATED CHICKEN WITH CELERIAC AND SORREL

Recipe by Chef Marc Meneau of L'Esperance, Saint-Père-Sous-Vézelay

In a small village in Burgundy you will find the charming village of Saint-Père-Sous-Vézelay.

L'Espérance, Saint-Père-Sous-Vézelay

In the distance, you will see the hill and the basilica. Nearby is a stream, and a garden filled with statues. A total of forty rooms are spread amongst a millhouse at the bottom of a field, the main house, and a nearby village house. The restaurant, L'Espérance, and Chef Marc Meneau, was awarded three Michelin stars for excellence. His approach, renowned for its purity and simplicity, for its subtlety and its originality, has won him wide acclaim as one of France's premier chefs. He has kindly agreed to create a special recipe for us, and we present it here. When in Burgundy, do not fail to plan a visit to his restaurant--it will be an unforgettable experience. Start with the chicken consommé with macaroons, then try the chaud-froid de homard en gelée, or the oysters in seawater gelatin. Desserts are unique and wonderful--for example the semolina tart with walnuts. An excellent experience in every way.

Serves 4

4	ounces	olive oil
1	chicken, preferably free-range, ~3 1/2 lb.	

For the marinade :

1	lemon -- juice only	10	cloves
1	bay leaf	1	teaspoon pepper
1	branch thyme	1	teaspoon tarragon
		4	cloves garlic -- peeled and crushed

For the Garniture:
  1/2   pound   celeriac -- cut in julienne
  1   teaspoon   horseradish purée
  1/4   cup   lowfat mayonnaise
  1   tablespoon   sherry vinegar
  1/4   pound   sorrel -- diced
        chopped parsley -- for garnish

Preparation of the marinade:
Reserve two tablespoons of the oil for cooking. Add the rest of the oil and all the marinade ingredients listed above (lemon juice through garlic) to a bowl, seal with plastic wrap. Infuse for a minimum of 2 hours. Remove the skin and bones from the chicken, cutting the chicken up in small pieces. Cut the white meat in 8 pieces, and also the dark meat in 8 pieces. Season them with salt and pepper. Marinate them 20 minutes at room temperature.

Preparation of the garniture:
Mix the celery root, the horseradish purée, and the mayonnaise. Season with salt and pepper.
Remove the pieces of poultry from the marinade. Add the olive oil to a non-stick sauté pan, bring to medium heat, add the chicken pieces and sauté until nicely golden. Set them aside and pour off any excess oil. Reheat the pan and add the sherry vinegar, scraping up any brown bits at the bottom of the pan. Add the marinade, and heat through. Adjust the seasoning with salt and pepper.

Presentation:
In the center of a pre-heated dinner plate, place 4 small bundles of diced sorrel seasoned with salt and pepper. Arrange four pieces of chicken on the sorrel, alternating white and then dark meat. Coat each piece with some of the hot marinade. Garnish with the julienne of celery root in mayonnaise, sprinkling with the chopped parsley.

491 calories.

DUCK

Magret de Canard, Sauce au Curry
BREAST OF DUCK IN CURRY SAUCE

This is what to do with those duck breasts leftover from the Cassoulet--but if you're like me--you'll be scouting markets for duck breasts to make this recipe because it's incredibly good, very easy, and won't unbalance the scales!

Serves 2

1		boneless duck breast, without skin -- about 10 ounces
2	cups	chicken stock
1	teaspoon	butter
1	teaspoon	flour
1/2	teaspoon	curry powder -- or more, to taste
1	teaspoon	mustard
2	tablespoons	sour cream, light

Remove all visible fat from the duck breast. Heat the chicken stock to boiling in a small saucepan, lower to a simmer, submerge the duck, and poach about 10 minutes. Reserve and keep warm. Spill off all but 1/2 cup of the stock, bring it to a simmer. Make a paste of the butter and flour (beurre manié), and add it little bits at a time, whisking, until the sauce thickens. Add the curry powder, the mustard, and season with salt and pepper. Remove from the heat. Whisk in the sour cream. Slice the duck breast on the diagonal, and fan out on two preheated dinner plates. Ladle the sauce over and around the duck breast. Serve immediately.

Duck Breast as a Chef's Suggestion on a blackboard in Lyon

249 calories per serving.

GUINEA FOWL

Pintadeau de la Drôme à la Vapeur de Gingembre
STEAMED GUINEA FOWL** IN GINGER SAUCE

**If guinea fowl is not readily available, use a small chicken such as a fryer.

Pic Hotel-Restaurant, Valence, France

Recipe by Chef Alain Pic of Pic Hotel-Restaurant, Valence, France

Pic is a family like no other. In 1891, Sophie Sahy married Eugène Pic who already owned a café, and began to cook, producing a unique and flavorful cuisine. André, her son, grew up by the stove, and learned his mother's secrets at an early age. To this he brought his own creativity, and by 1934 already had earned three Michelin stars. In 1936, he moved the restaurant to Valence on the National 7 road, and his son Jacques, born in 1932 eventually took the reins. Today, Jacques' son Alain heads up an extremely talented kitchen staff, where he and his close family members continue a family tradition over one hundred years old. The restaurant continues to be one of the finest in France; it still retains its Michelin three star rating. We wish to thank M. Alain Pic for his contribution to this book and his interest. While in Valence, try his Sea Bass with Caviar, or his Sautéed Langoustines in Olive Oil and Truffles. A wonderful and memorable experience!

3		carrots
2		leeks -- white part only
2	stalks	celery -- with leaves
1		guinea fowl or small chicken, skin removed, quartered
1	quart	chicken stock
1/3	ounce	ginger -- sliced
2	teaspoons	beurre manié*

*Beurre Manié: Take about 2 tablespoons flour and 2 tablespoons of butter and knead them

together into a paste. You will only use about 2 teaspoons of this mixture, but it's too hard to make up that small a quantity.

Peel the carrots and cut them in julienne (matchsticks). Wash the leeks very well, and cut the white part in julienne. Using a vegetable peeler, slice the strings off the celery stalks, remove and reserve the leaves, and cut them in julienne. Mix the vegetables and place them in the top of a steamer (a steamer basket in a casserole will do well).

If using chicken, cut each quarter in half. Arrange the guinea fowl (or chicken pieces) over the vegetables, then season them with salt and pepper. Pour the chicken stock in the bottom of the steamer, add the celery leaves, then the ginger. Bring the steamer to a boil, then lower the heat and cover the steamer. Cook about 35-40 minutes, or until the poultry is done. Keep the vegetables and meat hot, while you reduce the stock over high heat, uncovered, to about one quarter its original volume (1 cup). Strain, bring back to a simmer.

Knead the butter and flour together to form a paste (beurre manié), and slowly add bits of it to the stock until it thickens enough to coat the back of a spoon. Place the guinea fowl or chicken pieces in the center of four pre-heated dinner plates, surround them with the vegetables, and coat with the sauce. Serve hot.

298 calories.

HEN

Poularde Farcie, Sauce Crème a L'Ail
STUFFED HEN WITH GARLIC CREAM SAUCE

Serves 8

4	ounces	green olives-- pitted
3		ham slices, extra lean -- diced
3	cloves	garlic -- minced
1/2	pound	pork -- minced
1		egg
1/2	teaspoon	pepper
1	large	stewing hen
2	ribs	celery -- chopped roughly
1		carrot -- chopped roughly
1		onion -- chopped roughly
1		bouquet garni (parsley, thyme, and a bay leaf tied in cheesecloth)
1	cup	white wine

Sauce Crème a L'Ail:

20	cloves	garlic -- minced
6	ounces	skim milk
6	ounces	half and half
1	teaspoon	salt
1/4	teaspoon	white pepper

Blanch the olives, dry with paper towels, and chop coarsely. In a small mixing bowl, add the olives, the ham, the garlic, the pork, the egg, and, and the pepper. Mix thoroughly. Now, remove the giblets from the stewing hen and rinse the cavity thoroughly, then dry. Stuff the bird with the mixture, and truss. Place the hen in a large pot, and add the celery, carrots and onions, and the bouquet garni. Add the wine, and fill the pot with water just enough to cover the bird. Bring to a boil, reduce the heat to a slow simmer, and skim. Cover the pot, and cook about two hours or until the hen is tender. Thirty minutes or so before serving, start the sauce. Add the garlic and the skim milk to a small pot, and bring almost to a boil. Turn down the heat immediately (be careful--skim milk boils over quickly), and simmer gently 15 minutes, stirring occasionally. When the hen is done, remove the trussing string. Allow the bird to rest in a warm place, covered, while you finish the sauce. Pour the sauce mixture into a blender and purée well, then pour it back into its pot. Add the half and half, and bring almost back to the boiling point, once again reducing the heat quickly to allow the half and half to simmer. Season with salt and white pepper. Stirring, reduce by one-third.

Carve the hen, serving 1/8 to each person, along with some stuffing and then pour the sauce over each.

377 calories per serving with stuffing and sauce.

TURKEY

Turkey is one of those foods that the early American settlers brought back to the old country, and it has been eaten commonly in France since the 19th century. In recent years, perhaps owing to its relatively low cost, festive presentation, and low fat content, it has become surprisingly popular.

Roulâde de Dinde Farci
STUFFED ROLLED TURKEY

Serves 6
- 1 boneless turkey breast, about 2 pounds
- 1 egg
- 3 ounces turkey sausage -- skin discarded
- 4 ounces veal -- chopped
- 1/2 cup Gruyere cheese -- grated
- 2 cloves garlic -- minced
- 2 tablespoons olive oil
- 2 cups white wine
- 1 tablespoon cornstarch

Preheat the oven to 350°F. Lay the turkey breast on the cutting board and trim off all the skin, then turn the breast over and trim away enough meat from the thickest part to make 1/2 cup of

turkey meat. Dice this reserved turkey meat, and after placing the rest of the turkey breast in a large plastic baggie with two sides cut away, pound it slightly to flatten it into a rectangle. Discard the baggie.

In a medium sized bowl, combine the reserved diced turkey meat, the egg (beaten slightly), the turkey sausage meat, the veal, the cheese and the garlic. Place this mixture along one edge of the turkey breast, a little in from the edge, then roll the breast up jelly-roll fashion, and tie with kitchen string in several places.

Place a baking pan on the stove on medium heat, add the oil and the turkey roll, and brown on all sides. Pour off any excess oil, then add the wine and scrape up any brown bits to deglaze the pan. Cover the pan with aluminum foil and place it in the oven. Cook until a meat thermometer placed in the center reads 180°F, or about 1 1/4 hours. Remove turkey roll and keep warm, allowing it to rest about 10 minutes. Meanwhile, pour the cooking juices through a strainer into a small saucepan, and boil to reduce, if necessary, to about one cup of liquid. Make a slurry of 1 tablespoon of cornstarch and 2 tablespoons of cold water, and add it to the saucepan, cooking until the sauce thickens.

Remove the string from the turkey, slice, and serve with the sauce.

292 calories per person.

Fish

Filet de Saint-Pierre aux Tomates
FILET OF JOHN DORY WITH TOMATOES

Recipe by Chef Christian Morrisset, La Terrasse, Juan-les-Pins

In the magnificently renovated art deco Hotel Juana in Juan-les-Pins, sits a jewel of a restaurant, La Terrasse. It is one of the best restaurants on the Riviera owing to the enthusiasm and talent of its superb chef. Sit outside on the ivory-colored marble-floored terrace, overlooking a manicured garden of flowers and palm trees, and luxuriate in splendid French service. Soft, ivory table linens, beautiful china and silver, and soft music surround you.

A glimpse of La Terrasse, Juan-les-Pins (Antibes)

The food is superb, and the modest but handsome two-star Michelin chef Christian Morrisset is talented beyond his renown. You are apt to spot him easily because of his dashing handlebar mustache, either at the restaurant, or, if you go to the market in Cannes early in the morning. He'll be there to pick out the very best to serve that night. You might choose the scampi ravioli in a basil-flavored shellfish jus, or the plump turbot with truffles in a potato skin. The famous saddle of lamb cooked in its own clay casserole (and numbered for you to take home) is always a favorite. Whatever you select you won't go wrong.

We had the extreme pleasure of a tour of the market with Chef Morrisset, visiting his favorite suppliers and getting a glimpse of the true camaraderie that exists behind the scenes. He whipped up the above recipe for us, knowing that it will come out just right with many different kinds of fish, and that it offers the flavors of the Côte d'Azur without tipping the calorie scales too far.

Serves 4

4 fish fillets (John Dory is not easy to find on this side of the Atlantic--any flat fish will do)
1	tablespoon	olive oil
14	ounces	tomatoes -- sliced thick
1	bunch	basil leaves
3	ounces	olive oil
1	ounce	sherry vinegar
1	teaspoon	chives -- chopped fine
1/4	teaspoon	coriander
1	teaspoon	mint leaves -- chopped fine

Prepare a steamer, and steam the fish until just translucent (a bamboo steamer is fine; a covered sieve over a boiling pot of water will also do). Do not overcook or the fish will be dry. Place 1 tablespoon of olive oil in the bottom of a non-stick saucepan and heat on medium. Add tomatoes and cook, stirring occasionally, until soft. Remove any excess tomato skin, and keep warm. Purée the basil with the 3 ounces of olive oil and the sherry vinegar in a mini-chop or blender. Divide the tomatoes among 4 preheated dinner plates, and drizzle with the basil sauce. Place the fish in the center over the tomatoes, and sprinkle with the chives, coriander, and mint. Spoon up some of the sauce that has run out on the side of the plate, and spoon it over the fish.

Chef Christian Morrisset at the Market in Cannes

275 calories per serving.

Loup à la Moutarde
SEA BASS IN MUSTARD SAUCE

Mustard has been around since ancient times. The seeds were used as a treat with meat dishes for the Egyptians, and mustard was brought to Gaul by the Romans. By the 1400s, there was a guild of mustard makers, and the locale with the most success was Dijon. Today, about 50% of all French mustard is from Dijon. One special characteristic of Dijon mustard is that the ground mustard seed is dissolved in juice from unripe grapes, bringing a tartness to the mustard which is special and well appreciated.[1]

[1]Root, Waverly. The Food of France. Vintage Books, 1977.

Serves 4

1/4	cup	water
1	teaspoon	cornstarch
2	tablespoons	Dijon mustard
4	tablespoons	butter
1 1/2	pounds	sea bass fillets -- 4 fillets*
2	cups	fish stock
		chopped parsley & lemon slices for garnish

*Any firm-fleshed white fish will do well in this recipe, for example in addition to sea bass, try cod, grouper or red snapper.

Place the water and the cornstarch in a small saucepan, and whisk until combined. Place the pot on high heat, and just as it begins to boil, reduce the heat to a simmer and add the mustard. Season with salt and pepper. Cut the butter into small pieces and whisk it in slowly, continuing to whisk until you obtain a smooth sauce, about ten minutes. Do not allow the sauce to boil. Place the sauce in a pre-heated wide-mouthed vacuum bottle while you prepare the fish. Place the fish fillets in a non-stick sauté pan. Pour in the fish stock, and bring to a boil. Lower the heat to a simmer, and poach about 8 minutes. Lift the fish out carefully with a spider or large slotted spoon, dry with a paper towel if necessary, and place in the center of a pre-heated dinner plate. Ladle the mustard-butter sauce over and around it, and garnish with chopped parsley and lemon slices, if desired.

295 calories per serving.

Merou avec Tomate et Pernod
GROUPER WITH TOMATOES AND FENNEL

Serves 4

1		leek
1		fennel bulb
2	teaspoons	olive oil
2	cloves	garlic -- minced
1/4	cup	Pernod
28	ounces	tomatoes, diced -- (canned)
1/2	teaspoon	lemon zest -- grated
1		bay leaf
2	pounds	grouper fillets
2	tablespoons	fresh basil -- chopped
		fennel tops for garnish

Cut off about 1/3 of the green end of the leek, discard it, and then dice the rest of the leek and the fennel bulb. Add the oil to a large brazier or casserole, place on medium heat. Sauté the fennel and leek on all sides for about 5 minutes. Add the garlic, sauté one additional minute. Add the Pernod, turn the heat to high and bring to a boil. Then add the tomatoes including the liquid from the can, the lemon zest, and the bay leaf. Bring all of this to a boil, then cover and lower the heat, simmering for about 20-25 minutes stirring occasionally until the vegetables are soft. Season with salt and pepper. Add the grouper to the pot, allowing it to sink into the sauce. Simmer gently, uncovered, until the fish is just cooked through, perhaps 7-9 minutes. Remove the fish and keep warm. Remove and discard the bay leaf. Bring the sauce to a boil and reduce until thickened, about 3 minutes, then stir in the chopped basil. Plate the fillets, spoon the sauce over them, and garnish with a few sprigs from the top of the fennel.

275 calories.

Mousse de Saumon
SALMON MOUSSE

Serves 4

15	ounces	salmon -- canned	2	small	zucchini
2		eggs		dill for garnish	
2		lemons	4	teaspoons	mayonnaise,lowfat
2	teaspoons	lemon juice	Frisée, mâche, or other varietal lettuce		

Separate the eggs, placing the yolks and lemon juice in a blender. Give a few pulses just to combine well, then add the salt and pepper. Drain the salmon, mash it, and add it to the blender. Purée thoroughly until entirely smooth. Using an electric mixer or wire whisk, beat the egg whites to soft peaks, then fold in the salmon mixture. Spoon into individual ramekins (straight-sided custard cups), pre-sprayed with vegetable oil spray, and refrigerate about 1 hour. Preheat the oven to 350°F. Then place the ramekins into a pan of hot water that comes halfway up their sides, and bake for 30 minutes (when trying to bake something in a water bath, it's often more convenient to put the ramekins into an empty pan in the oven, and then pour in boiling water from a kettle).

Meanwhile, slice the zucchini thinly, and simmer just until tender. Chill. Cut the lemons into

quarters. When the mousse is finished, run a knife around the inside of each ramekin and unmold the salmon mousse onto the plates. Decorate with the lemon wedges, the mayonnaise, the dill and the zucchini and serve on a bed of lettuce.

One possible interpretation of this recipe is to chop up the dill and mix with the mayonnaise as dill mayonnaise is a nice accompaniment. Another possibility is to spread the mayonnaise over the entire surface of the mousse, and then decorate. It's very tasty this way, but you may need a bit more mayo.

A variation on this dish is to use canned or cooked chicken in place of the fish--very easy and a whole new taste. Try making individual molds and then covering them with chaud-froid sauce (see recipe), then decorating them with bits of red and yellow pepper, thin slices of olive, or anything your imagination suggests.

179 calories per serving.

Quenelles de Poisson
QUENELLES OF FISH

These are very light fish dumplings and can be made with any white fish that is available, as they would be with the catch of the day in France. Other fish can be used, such as salmon, tuna, or even chicken or veal, with interesting if not typically traditional results. They are served with a sauce which can vary to suit your taste. Quenelles are from Lyon in the Rhône, and traditionally are made of pike, and called Quenelles de Brochet. Quenelles are a heavenly sort of fish cake (seems criminal to call them by such plebeian terms) served with a variety of sauces, such as the well-known Sauce Nantua. Nantua, a village about 40 minutes northwest of Lyon, is known for its freshwater crayfish, and

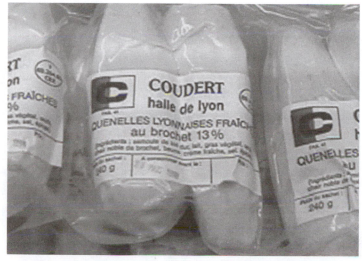

Quenelles for sale at the market, the "Halle de Lyon." Yours will be better!

Nantuans frequently add crayfish to the quenelle itself, as well as serving it in crayfish sauce. Sauce Nantua is a delicious sauce made of béchamel with crayfish stock and crayfish butter, and a little cognac. We offer a somewhat less caloric version--check under Béchamel Sauce. It would do very well here instead of the velouté.

Serves 4

   1 pound pike fillets -- or fillets of almost any white fish (fresh or frozen)
   1/2   pound *shrimp, or crayfish -- shelled, raw (fresh or frozen)
   1   tablespoon scallions -- minced
   1/8   teaspoon nutmeg
   1/3   cup nonfat sour cream
   2   tablespoons bread crumbs
   3/4   cup egg substitute such as *Eggbeaters*®
   1/2   teaspoon lemon juice

Quenelles of shrimp (see recipe above) on sale at the hypermarket, Lyon

   2 cups Velouté sauce for fish (*see recipe and note quantity--this is double the usual amount of sauce for 4*)

     *Optional, but I strongly recommend it--the Quenelles aux Crevettes (shrimp) we had in Lyon were my favorites--see picture below. If using crayfish, be careful not to accidentally buy the ones with Creole seasoning--only use unseasoned crayfish!

Make the sauce first according to the directions in our recipe, and place it in a pre-heated thermos bottle, or in the refrigerator.

Place the fish, and shellfish if using, scallions, nutmeg and a little salt and pepper in the bowl of a food processor, and pulse just until puréed, about a minute. Add the non-fat sour cream and bread crumbs and pulse for a few seconds just until combined. If necessary, scrape down the

Quenelle de Brochet in Sauce Nantua as prepared at the Brasserie de l'Hotel de Ville, Nantua, France. Yours will look just like this!

sides of the bowl with a rubber spatula, then add the egg substitute and pulse a few times again, just enough to combine the ingredients. Scrape out the purée into a bowl, and chill for half an hour.

Set about a quart of water on the stove to boil in a non-stick sauté pan, add the lemon juice, and a tablespoon of salt. Divide the batter in four portions. Form each portion of the batter into a log as shown in the photos, using a couple of rubber spatulas, or by rolling a scoopful of batter in saran wrap and shaping it into a log. After shaping, you should re-chill them for 15 to 30 minutes. Lower the heat until the water is *barely* at a simmer (bubbling of water may cause the quenelles to fall apart), and gently slide in a quenelle. After about four to five minutes, turn it once very gently (use two spatulas), and allow it to poach about two to three minutes more, or until just firm. Poach the quenelles no more than two at a time to avoid overcrowding them in the pan. You can refrigerate the quenelles at this point, if you wish.

When ready to serve, preheat the oven to 425°F, set each quenelle into an ovenproof serving dish such as a gratin dish, ladle 1/2 cup of sauce over it, and place in the top third of the oven until hot and bubbly. Baste quenelle with sauce. Then, turn the oven to broil for just a few minutes until it begins to turn golden brown. Garnish with some slices of lemon, some chopped fresh parsley, and serve.

Because the water content of fish, especially if frozen, varies, the batter may need a little more sour cream if too thick, or binding with an egg yolk or a few more breadcrumbs if too thin.

322 calories each, with the sauce.

Page 144

Ragoût Provençal de Poisson
FISH STEW FROM PROVENCE

Serves 6

Rouille (see recipe)
3 cloves garlic minced
1   teaspoon olive oil
1   tablespoon tomato paste
4   bunches fennel stalks
1   bouquet garni (thyme, parsley, and a bay leaf tied in a cheesecloth)
2   teaspoons saffron
4   cups   fish stock (see recipe, "Fumet de Poisson")
2 1/4   pounds fish fillets*
3 large potatoes, boiled and sliced
12 French baguette slices, toasted

* Use fish such as sea bass, red snapper, monkfish or rockfish. Try to get several kinds.

First, make the rouille: See recipe for rouille under sauces.

In a soup kettle, sauté the minced garlic in the olive oil for one to two minutes. Add the tomato paste, the fennel, the bouquet garni, the saffron and the fish stock. Simmer 15 minutes and remove the bouquet garni and the fennel stalks. Cut the fish fillets in 2" pieces, and add them to the pot. Simmer about 10 minutes until fish is cooked.

To serve, place about 6 ounces of mixed fish fillets in the center of a soup plate. Add the sliced potatoes, and two rounds of toasted baguette spread with the rouille. Pour in the hot broth, and serve immediately.

425 calories, with the bread and rouille.

Did you know that saffron is made of the collected stamens of a small purple crocus flower? It takes 14,000 flowers to provide enough for one ounce of saffron. That's why saffron is expensive.

Roulades de Poisson
ROULADES OF FISH

Serves 4

12 ounces fish fillets*
1/2 cup half and half
6 ounces smoked salmon

For the Sauce:
1 teaspoon butter
1 teaspoon flour
1/2 cup fish stock (see recipe)
1/2 cup skim milk
1/2 lemon, juice only

For the Julienne:
2 ribs fennel
2 carrots
2 ribs celery
2 small zucchini
2 tablespoons oil
chopped chervil for garnish

*Any firm fleshed white fish can be used, from whitefish to catfish.

In a food processor or blender, purée the fish with salt and pepper. With the machine running, add the half and half gradually. On a piece of wax paper divide the fish paste into four parts. Form the paste into log shapes. Drape the salmon over the logs. Refrigerate while you make the sauce.

Allow the butter to come to room temperature. Knead the butter and flour together to make a paste (beurre manié). Bring the fish stock to a boil, and let it cook 5 minutes. Add the milk and cook 5 more minutes. Add the beurre manié bit by bit to thicken the sauce. Strain if necessary. Season with salt and pepper, add the lemon juice, and keep warm but do not boil (a vacuum bottle is ideal for this). Now, make the julienne.

Peel all the vegetables except the zucchini. Cut them into julienne (matchsticks), including the zucchini. In a medium saucepan, heat the oil, and add all the vegetables except the zucchini. Sauté slowly, covered. Stir occasionally. After about 15 minutes, add the zucchini.

While the vegetables are cooking, carefully put the fish logs into a steamer and steam eight to ten minutes. Place each roulade on a heated dinner plate, ladle a little fish sauce over each one, and decorate with the julienne of vegetables and a few leaves of chopped chervil. Serve immediately.

290 calories, with the vegetables.

Saumon au Beurre Blanc et à l'Aneth
SALMON IN A DILL BEURRE BLANC SAUCE

Beurre blanc ("white butter") is traditionally thought of as a hard sauce to make, because it is a tenuously bound emulsion that is difficult to make, and even more difficult to hold until serving time. In my version, the sauce holds beautifully and tastes perfectly with the addition of a secret ingredient that solves the difficulty--cornstarch. A second secret is the vacuum bottle (Thermos®-type) that will hold a difficult sauce perfectly hot until serving time without risking overheating and breaking the sauce. Preheat the vacuum bottle by filling it with boiling water, which you pour out just before filling with sauce. A wide-mouth type is easiest for ladling out the sauce at serving time, but if yours is narrow-necked, you can simply pour the sauce out. While the sauce will stay hot and in perfect condition for two hours or more, don't try to hold it longer than an hour or so because of safety concerns.

This recipe is definitely not low fat, so reserve it for those times when you need something really rich. However, at 433 calories it will fit into most people's diet plans at least once in a while. There's just no substitute for the rich taste of butter in the sauce. Of course you could choose a lower calorie fish, or poach it instead of roasting it in oil....

Serves 4

For the Beurre Blanc:
    2 shallots -- or 1 small red onion
    1/2 cup white wine
        pinch of white pepper
    1 teaspoon cornstarch
    7 tablespoons butter
    1 teaspoon dill
        fresh dill for garnish
For the fish:
    24   ounces salmon fillets
    1   tablespoon olive oil

Make the sauce:

 Peel and chop the shallots. Pour the wine into a saucepan, add the shallots and cook over moderately high heat until reduced to about one ounce. Strain and discard the shallots. Return the liquid to the saucepan, season with salt and white pepper, and whisk in the cornstarch carefully to avoid lumps. After reheating to the simmering point, add one tablespoon of the butter and whisk in. Lower the heat to low and add the rest of the butter, one tablespoon at a time, whisking constantly, until all the butter is incorporated. Add the dill. Pour the sauce into the preheated vacuum bottle, and close tightly.

Preheat the oven to 375°F. Add the oil to an ovenproof non-stick sauté pan, and place over medium heat on the stove. Place the salmon fillets in the pan, skin side down. Season with salt and pepper. Now, the raw fish has the typical reddish translucent hue of uncooked salmon. As it cooks, its color changes to what I call "pink", and it becomes opaque. Watch carefully, and when the opaque pink color has come up about half the thickness of the fish, transfer it to the oven and bake about 10 minutes. Do not turn the fish over at any point.

Slide the salmon into the center of a preheated dinner plate, and ladle the dill beurre blanc out of the vacuum bottle onto the fish, about one ounce per portion. Garnish with fresh dill, if desired, and serve.

433 calories.

Seafood
Crevettes à la Maison
HOME-STYLE SHRIMP

Serves 4

4	turnips, peeled, diced, boiled until tender
1	tablespoon olive oil
2	cups fish stock (see recipe)
1	pound shrimp, whole, unpeeled
1	carrot peeled & chopped
1/2	cup leeks, chopped
1	bouquet garni (thyme, parsley, bay leaf tied in cheesecloth)
2	teaspoons soy sauce
2	tablespoons cornstarch
4	sprigs flat-leaf parsley

Place the oil in a sauté pan, and when hot add all but 1/2 cup of the diced turnips, and turn the heat down to low. Sauté them slowly, turning occasionally, for about 5 to 10 minutes until golden brown.

Meanwhile, take 1/2 cup of the fish stock and pour it into a saucepan, bring it to a boil, add the shrimp, and simmer about 3 minutes until the shrimp turn pink. Remove the shrimp and allow them to cool slightly. Peel the shrimp, and reserve. Add the shrimp shells back into the saucepan, add the remaining stock and the bouquet garni, and simmer 15 minutes. Strain the stock and reserve.

Pass the remaining turnips, the carrot, and the leek through a vegetable juicer, and add the juice to the stock. Add the soy sauce and reduce to 2/3 cup. Season with salt and pepper. Add the cornstarch to 2 tablespoons of cold water, and whisk into a slurry. Add to the sauce, and bring to a simmer just long enough to thicken. Add the sautéed turnips and the shrimp to the sauce, warm through, and serve garnished with the parsley.

234 calories

Homard à L'Americaine
LOBSTER AMERICAINE

Some say the name of this dish is a corruption of Amoricaine, making reference to the Amorica, the old name for Brittany. This seems unlikely to me. This dish is certainly of Meditteranean origin, as can be guessed from its ingredients. Tomatoes were hardly known outside that region until the nineteenth century. During the mid-1800's, this dish was called Lobster à la Provençal; I believe the term Americaine referred to a simpler type of poached lobster dish. Where the switch in names occurred is a matter for speculation. According to Larousse Gastronomique, Escoffier believed the dish was exported by a chef from Nice to America, from which it was reimported back to France. This theory seems closer to the truth. Therefore, he thought the name was a corruption of "American". Whatever the actual origins of this dish, it is a truly classic French dish, which is spectacular in its interpretation here--traditional--yet yours to enjoy.

Serves 6

3		lobsters -- 1 1/2 lbs. each
1/4	cup	olive oil
1/2	cup	onion -- finely chopped
1	clove	garlic -- finely chopped
1/4	cup	brandy
1/4	cup	sherry
14 1/2	ounces	canned tomatoes -- diced
1		bay leaf
1		bouquet garni
2	tablespoons	butter
4	tablespoons	flour
2	cups	fish stock (see recipe, "Fumet de Poisson")
2	tablespoons	tomato paste
1	pinch	saffron
		salt and cayenne pepper
		chopped chives for garnish

Steam lobsters 5 minutes, remove the meat and chill. Chop the lobster shells using a cleaver. Add the olive oil to a soup kettle, turn the heat to medium, add the shells, the onions and the garlic and sauté 5 minutes. Add the brandy and sherry and allow to boil about 2 minutes. Add the diced tomatoes, the bay leaf and the bouquet garni. Turn down to low while you make the velouté, as follows.

Melt the butter in a saucepan. Stir in the flour, and reduce the heat. Keep stirring and cooking for a few minutes to get rid of the floury taste, then stir in the fish stock gradually, until well combined. Then add this velouté back into the soup kettle, and simmer about 5 minutes. Strain back into the saucepan, add the tomato paste, the saffron, and simmer until thickened. Season with salt and cayenne pepper. Chop the lobster meat into bite-sized pieces, and add it to the sauce. When warmed through, serve, garnishing with chopped chives. As a suggestion, serve with boiled rice or couscous.

290 calories per portion.

Lobster is low in calories, and can be enjoyed regularly if prices permit. I would suggest foregoing the boring drawn butter, and enjoying the lobster with a sauce from our sauce section. When you have lobster, save and freeze the shells. Then, defrost them at your leisure in the microwave, prepare the Americaine sauce as above, and use it to poach any non-oily fish such as filets of sole, flounder, shrimp, or even crawfish tails (fresh or frozen). The flavor of the lobster permeates the dish, you obtain a wonderful sauce, and all this from the parts you always threw away!

Homard à la Nage
LOBSTER COOKED IN ITS OWN BROTH

Recipe by Chef Olivier Roellinger of Les Maisons de Bricourt

Chef Olivier Roellinger prepared this recipe for us from Cancale, France, which is a small fishing port situated between Mont Saint-Michel and Saint-Malo in Brittany. His food is described as "a cuisine of expression between land and sea." This is where he presides over a magnificent restaurant called "Les Maisons de Bricourt," located in his own childhood home. His restaurant is well known to lovers of his "Homard aux Saveurs des Iles," and his "Carré d'Agneau de Prés Salés." Les Rimains is a 6-room cottage facing the Cancale oyster beds, and the Châteaux Richeux is a charming seafood bistro overlooking the Mont-Saint-Michel bay.

Serves 4

1		carrot
1		leek -- white part only
1		shallot
1/4	stalk	celery
3	ounces	butter -- cold
1	cup	white wine
1	cup	chicken stock
1		orange -- zest only
5	seeds	fenugreek -- if available*
1	teaspoon	coriander -- ground
1	bunch	chervil
2	sprigs	parsley
1	sprig	thyme
4	seeds	cumin
3	leaves	tarragon
4	small	lobsters
2	teaspoons	salt
1	dash	Cayenne pepper
		lemon juice -- to taste

* Fenugreek is often available in the US in health food stores; leave it out if you can't find it.

Basic preparation:

Wash the carrots and the leek well, mince them, along with the shallot and the celery. Melt one tablespoon of the butter in a sauté pan, and sauté until translucent, then add the wine. Bring to the boil, and let it reduce about 5 minutes, then add the chicken stock and a cup of water. Add the orange zest, the fenugreek (if using) and the coriander. Bring to the boil, reduce the heat, and simmer 30 minutes (it must be a very slow simmer, if not you will allow too much liquid to evaporate). Allow to cool, and pass through a fine sieve.

At time of serving:

Reserve some of the chervil for garnish. Chop the rest along with the parsley, the thyme, cumin and the tarragon. Reserve. Bring the previously prepared broth to a boil. Add the lobsters, and close tightly with a lid to steam. After about 8 minutes, remove them. Dice the remaining cold butter, and add it and the chopped herbs to the broth, mixing well to melt the butter. After infusing for about 4 minutes, strain the broth. Check the seasoning, and add salt, Cayenne pepper, and lemon juice as needed to taste. Shell the lobsters if desired, and add them back to the broth. Stirring occasionally, bring the temperature up to simmering. Serve each lobster with about a half cup of broth, sprinkling the lobsters with the reserved chervil.

Note: Be sure you have about 2 cups of liquid at the end. If you have boiled away too much, add water to make up the 2 cups. If you have too much, boil it down to about 2 cups. Consider serving some bread with this dish--it's great to sop up the broth!

389 calories per serving.

Les Coquilles Saint-Jacques à la Sauce Persil
SCALLOPS IN PARSLEY SAUCE

Recipe by Chef Bernard Loiseau, Restaurant La Côte d'Or, Saulieu

A high profile chef, Bernard Loiseau has once again turned his focus to his cooking. Despite great personal financial strain, he has completely renovated his hotel and restaurant, so that it is now a Mecca for all those making the culinary rounds in France. The dining room is elegant but not stuffy, with its wood-beamed ceiling and lavish windows, its tile floor and its tall silver candlesticks. Just watch the other patrons carefully studying the menu, and comparing the merits of one dish against another. Sample the rouget with carrot galette, or the John Dory with oyster vinaigrette. Many come to try the famous poularde truffée à la vapeur; this steamed chicken with truffled basmati rice is guaranteed to be one of the most aromatic dishes you've ever tasted.

Born in 1951 at Chamalières, chef Loiseau won his first Michelin star in 1977, and his third in 1991. Also in '91 he won the chef of the year award in the professional French magazine," Le Chef." He has been reviewed by the New York Times and the Smithsonian. He was named to the French Legion of Honor in 1995, and in

1996 his statue was added to the wax museum *Grevin* in Paris as one of only two statues representing cuisine. He has graciously provided us with a recipe he has created, which exemplifies how much is possible using a small number of ingredients, within strict calorie limits, when your imagination is as broad as Chef Loiseau's.

Serves 4

1   large bunch   Italian parsley
1/2   cup milk   (or less)
3   drops lemon juice, or so
1 1/2   pounds sea scallops   (preferably "diver's scallops" available in specialty fish markets-- these are large sea scallops without preservative chemicals)
2   tablespoons   olive oil

Reserve about 4 sprigs of parsley as a garnish. Discard the stems from the rest of the parsley, and plunge the leaves into a pot of boiling water for three minutes. Then drain and plunge them into an ice water bath immediately. Drain again, and dry on paper towels. Using a blender or food processor, purée the leaves. Scrape them into a small mixing bowl, and add a few drops of lemon juice and, while stirring, only enough milk to create a sauce. Place the mixture back in the blender and purée for several minutes until nearly smooth. Heat slowly to warm, but do not allow to simmer or boil. Keep warm in a vacuum bottle.

Meanwhile, season the scallops with salt and pepper. Place a non-stick sauté pan on high heat, and add the two tablespoons of olive oil. When very hot (but not smoking), add the scallops. Sauté quickly to a golden--thirty seconds to a minute or so per side. Remove the scallops immediately to absorbent paper. Spoon some of the parsley sauce in the center of a pre-heated dinner plate, then arrange the scallops around the sauce. Garnish with the reserved parsley sprigs, perhaps some lemon if desired, and serve immediately.

230 calories per serving.

About Mussels

Mussels are great fun to use, tasty, and fairly available (sometimes frozen) even in more remote parts of our country. They are also a nice change from the usual seafood, and are very common in France.

Always check fresh mussels before preparation. Wash and remove any attached material (beards). Tap any whose shells are not tightly closed, and if they do not even attempt to close their shells, discard them.

Moules Farcies
STUFFED MUSSELS

This recipe is a bit of work, what with stuffing and tying up each mussel, but it's a *great* tasting recipe, low in calories, and not at all difficult!

Serves 2

18 mussels
1/4 pound turkey sausage
2 tablespoons mixed fresh herbs --minced
2 cloves garlic -- minced
3 tablespoons olive oil
1 cup Sauce Tomate (see recipe), or use a prepared sauce such as *Ragú Lite*®
1 cup rice -- boiled
2 tablespoons fresh parsley -- minced

The mussels have been stuffed and tied, and placed in the pan, ready to cook

Wash and debeard the mussels. Using a clam knife, open the mussels and drain. Mix the sausage meat with the garlic and the herbs. Spoon the sausage mixture into the mussels, about a spoonful each. Close the mussels, and tie each with kitchen string. Place the oil in a sauté pan, heat over medium heat, and sauté the mussels about 4 minutes. Then turn them over with tongs and continue cooking about 4 more minutes. Now, turn the heat down very low, and cook about 15 minutes, turning the mussels from time to time. Pour off any excess oil, and turn the heat up to high. Add the tomato sauce, and cook another ten to twelve minutes. Cut off the strings. Serve over the cooked rice, garnishing with the chopped parsley.

Moules Farcies with rice, ready to serve!

327 calories, including the rice.

Moules Maison
HOME-STYLE MUSSELS

Serves 2

1   tablespoon olive oil
1/4 cup   onions -- diced
4   cloves garlic -- minced
1/2 cup   vermouth, dry
1/2 can whole tomatoes -- diced— about 8 ozs.
2 dozen mussels
1/4 cup   parsley -- chopped
1   teaspoon cornstarch
1   cup fish stock (or chicken stock, if handier)
1   tablespoon half and half
       parsley for garnish

In a non-stick sauté pan over medium heat, add the oil, and when hot, the onions. Cook until they turn translucent. Then add the garlic, cook one more minute, and add the vermouth and the tomatoes, stirring to scrape up any brown bits at the bottom of the pan. Add the stock, bring to a simmer, add the mussels, and cover.

When all the mussels have opened, remove them from the pot and keep them warm. Add the chopped parsley to the pot. Whisk the cornstarch with the half and half to form a slurry, and add, stirring, to thicken the sauce. Season with salt and pepper. Place a dozen mussels into a large, pre-heated soup dish, and pour the sauce over them.

282 calories per serving.

Desserts

CLAFOUTIS

A classic French dish, easy to make, and extremely versatile. Fix a cherry clafoutis (classic), or use apples or whatever fruit is fresh at the market. Use it as a dessert for the family, for company, or fix it with cherry tomatoes as a lunch or side dish. Easy to make!

Serves 6

    1 1/4 cups milk
    1/4 cup sugar
    3 eggs
    1 tablespoon vanilla
    1/8 teaspoon salt
    2/3 cup flour
    3 cups cherries -- pitted
        confectioner's sugar for garnish

Prepare whichever fruit you are using:

Cherries: 3 cups pitted black cherries either fresh, canned or frozen. If canned or frozen, drain

well. Cherries may be allowed to steep in 1/4 cup cognac and 1/4 cup sugar. If you choose this method, omit the milk and the sugar in the recipe.

Apples: 3 cups of peeled, cored and sliced apples (1/4") thick. Sauté in 3 tablespoons of butter till golden brown, steep in Calvados and 1/4 cup sugar and 1/4 teaspoon cinnamon. Omit the sugar and the milk from the recipe.

And the same recipe can be used to prepare a vegetable course, using cherry tomatoes: Use 3 cups of cherry tomatoes, omit sugar and confectioner's sugar.

Cherry Tomato Clafoutis—a quick and easy lunch or appetizer

Preheat oven to 350°F. Add first six ingredients to a mixing bowl (milk through flour) and mix well 2 minutes by hand or with an electric mixer. Pour a thin layer of the batter into a 7-8 cup baking dish or pie plate which has been sprayed with pan spray, and place over low heat or in the oven until set. Spread fruit over the set batter in the dish, and pour the remaining batter over the fruit. Bake about 35 to 45 minutes until a toothpick inserted in the center comes out clean. Sprinkle with confectioner's sugar if desired, and serve warm.

Cherry: 183 cal
Apple: 210 calories
Cherry tomato: 143 calories

Crêpes aux Framboises
RASPBERRY CRÊPES

Serves 4

1/2	package	vanilla pudding mix, sugar-free, fat free (4 tablespoons)
1/2	cup	skim milk
2	ounces	raspberry jam -- melted
8		crêpes (see recipe)
1/2	pound	raspberries, frozen -- with juice
		confectioner's sugar
		mint leaves
		raspberries for garnish

Mix vanilla pudding and skim milk for 2 minutes with an electric beater, or by hand. Fold in raspberry jam. Fold in raspberries, reserving some for garnish, and divide among the 8 crêpes. Roll up crêpes, jelly roll style. Dust with confectioner's sugar and serve, or, after dusting run under the broiler for a moment to glaze. Serve one or two crêpes per person. Garnish with mint leaves and raspberries.

For a special presentation, make a design with raspberry coulis and Crème Anglaise (see recipes under basics) on the plate.

105 calories per crêpe.

CRÊPES SUZETTE

This is a very festive dessert that can be prepared in the kitchen or tableside. I always like to do it tableside in the dining room because it's very impressive, although not very difficult (but you might want to have a practice session beforehand). Set up custard cups or ramekins as your *mise en place*—that is—put all your prepared ingredients in them and set them on a tray near the dining table. Use a portable camp stove or buffet burner as your heat source, just be sure it's got enough power to boil water. And be sure to use a sauté pan that looks clean on the outside, too, as your guests will be looking at it. Perform each step with as much flair and show as you think the occasion demands, less at a barbecue, more in the dining room. Turn the lights down low for a little drama before igniting the pan. Enjoy!

Serves 6

1	orange	
1/2	lemon	
4	tablespoons	butter
4	tablespoons	sugar
1/4 cup	Grand Marnier	
1/4 cup	brandy	
4	teaspoons	sugar for garnish
12	crêpes (see recipe under Basics), folded in quarters	

Either zest the orange with a zester, or peel the outer skin only with a vegetable peeler (leaving the bitter white pith behind), and cut it in 1/8" strips (julienne). Boil the zest one or two minutes, drain, and set aside. Juice the orange and the 1/2 lemon, and set aside.

Place the butter in the sauté pan tableside, if desired, and melt over low heat. Add the sugar, orange and lemon juices, and mix over low heat. Add the zest. Cook until butter and sugar have dissolved, the bring up to a boil. Add the Grand Marnier, bring back to a boil.

Place the crêpes in the sauce. Pour in half the brandy, and heat the other half in a ladle. If using a gas heat source, tip the ladle slightly so that the brandy ignites (taking care to keep hair and face away). If using an electric heat source, ignite the brandy with a match. Ladle it onto the crêpes quickly. Shake the pan vigorously until the flames subside. Serve 3 crêpes to a portion, ladling the sauce over them, and garnishing with a little granulated sugar and the orange zest. Add mint leaves if desired.

266 calories per two crêpe serving including the sauce and brandy.

Mille Feuilles aux Bananes
BANANA NAPOLEONS

A very grand dessert that is truly elegant, easy to make and with an incredibly low calorie count.

Serves 6

butter-flavored pan spray
4   sheets phyllo dough -- thawed
8   teaspoons sugar
1 1/4 cups skim milk
4   medium bananas -- sliced 1/4" thick
3   tablespoons sugar and fat free vanilla pudding mix, (1/2 large pkg.)
1 1/2 cups fat free prepared dessert topping such as *Cool Whip*®
    confectioner's sugar
    mint leaves
    strawberries or raspberries for garnish

Preheat the oven to 400° F. Cut a piece of parchment paper to fit a cookie sheet. Spray the cookie sheet with pan spray, and adhere the parchment paper to the cookie sheet. Spray the parchment paper with pan spray. Unwrap a package of phyllo dough and remove one sheet, placing it on a cutting board. Lay a piece of plastic wrap over the remaining unused sheets, and a damp kitchen towel over that. Returning to the phyllo sheet on the cutting board, spray it all over with pan spray, using about 2 good sprays. Take two teaspoons of sugar in your hand, and from a height of about 1 1/2 feet, sprinkle them all over the phyllo dough, covering as evenly as you can. Repeat this maneuver with the next 3 phyllo sheets, re-covering the stack each time to keep the unused phyllo sheets moist. Using a sharp knife, cut the stack of 4 prepared phyllo sheets into 12 equal rectangles, discarding scraps. Place the rectangles on the parchment paper, and bake 3-5 minutes until golden brown. Depending on the size of your cookie sheet, this may be done in one or two batches. Set aside to cool.

Pour the skim milk into a blender, and add one sliced banana. Turn the blender on to purée, then add the pudding mix and purée another minute or so. Pour into a mixing bowl and chill at least 30 minutes. The fold in the *Cool Whip*® until well mixed.

To serve, place one phyllo rectangle on a dessert plate. Spoon on about 1/2 cup of the banana cream custard, and top with the slices of 1/2 banana. Set a second phyllo rectangle on top of the banana slices, and dust well with confectioner's sugar. Garnish with mint leaves and berries. Serve immediately.

157 calories each.

ORANGES À LA GRAND MARNIER

Serves 4

4	oranges: three peeled & sliced, one whole
1/4 cup	sugar
1/2 cup	Grand Marnier
	mint leaves for garnish

Using a vegetable peeler, remove the zest (colored part of the peel) of the whole orange, avoiding the bitter white pith. Remove the remaining white pith from the orange with a knife, and discard the pith. Then slice and reserve the resulting orange along with the three already sliced. If the underside of any of the zest strips has much pith, slice it away with a paring knife. Julienne the zest into 1/4" wide strips, about 2" long. Place the strips into a small saucepan with a cup of water, boil for 3 minutes, then strain discarding the liquid. Add 1/4 cup water to the saucepan, then add the sugar and stir to combine. Add the julienne, and boil until the liquid reduces and becomes syrupy. Remove the candied julienne with a slotted spoon and set aside on a dish to cool.

Place all of the orange slices and the Grand Marnier in a zip-lock type plastic bag, eject air and seal. Allow to infuse for two hours or more. Arrange the orange slices attractively on four dessert plates, and garnish with the candied orange zest and the mint leaves.

144 calories per serving.

Poires Rôties
ROASTED CARAMELIZED PEARS

Serves 6

1	cup	Sauterne wine
1	teaspoon	vanilla extract
6	pears -- peeled, cored, halved
3	tablespoons	sugar (divided)
1	tablespoon	butter
	mint leaves	

Preheat the oven to 450°F. Pour the wine in a large ovenproof fry pan, add the vanilla, and bring to a boil over medium heat. Remove from the heat and add the pears, cored side up. Sprinkle with half the sugar and place in the oven. Bake 10 minutes, turn the pears cut side down, sprinkle with remaining sugar and dot with butter. Continue baking an additional 25 minutes or so. Remove from the oven, take the pears out of the fry pan and reserve, allowing to cool slightly. Reduce the sauce until syrupy on top of the stove. Arrange two pear halves in each of six dessert dishes, and drizzle with the sauce. Garnish with mint leaves. Serve warm.

157 calories.

Pouding au Pain
FRENCH BREAD PUDDING

French bread can be a baker's miracle when it comes straight from the oven, piping hot, with that crusty exterior and delicious, tender crumb inside. But like all good things, it doesn't last long. By tomorrow morning, it's as useful as a brittle baseball bat. Here's what to do with it when it gets stale.

Serves 6

For the Pudding:
  2   cups skim milk
  1   vanilla bean
  1/2 cup egg substitute, such as *Eggbeaters*®
  1/2 cup sugar
  1/2 teaspoon cinnamon
  3 French baguette slices -- stale
  1   apple -- peeled & cored
  3   egg whites

For the sauce:
  3/4   cup milk, 1% lowfat
  2   tablespoons sugar
  1/4   cup Calvados -- or brandy
  1   tablespoon   cornstarch
       pan spray, sugar for dusting

Preheat the oven to 325°F. Slice the vanilla bean lengthwise and place it and the milk in a small saucepan. Heat to just below boiling, allow to cool slightly. Meanwhile, in a bowl add the egg substitute, 1/4 cup of the sugar, and the cinnamon. Whisk together, then add the hot milk slowly while whisking to prevent the eggs from cooking. Cube the French bread, and soak in the egg and milk mixture. Pour it all in a food processor, purée and reserve. Purée the apple in the food processor, and fold into the custard. Beat the egg whites using a mixer until soft peaks form, then gradually beat in the remaining 1/4 cup of sugar. Fold into the custard mixture, and then turn into a 1 quart mold sprayed with pan spray and dusted with sugar. Place the mold in a pan of hot water that comes halfway up its side, and bake 50 to 60 minutes until a toothpick inserted in the center comes out clean. Allow to cool slightly while preparing the sauce.

Bring the milk and sugar for the sauce almost to the boiling point. Mix the cornstarch with the cold Calvados, and add to the milk. Bring to a boil, reduce the heat and simmer until thickened.

Unmold the pudding and serve with the sauce.

222 calories per serving.

Pêches au Vin Blanc
PEACHES IN WHITE WINE

Serves 6

1	cup white wine
1/4	cup sugar
1	vanilla bean -- split
6	medium peaches, freestone -- peeled, pitted & halved (about 2 pounds)
	mint leaves

Add wine and sugar to a large frying pan, and bring to a boil on medium heat. Add vanilla bean, scraping seeds into the pan. Place the peaches in the pan, cut sides down, and simmer 5 minutes (more or less depending on the ripeness of the peaches) until softened. Turn the peaches over and simmer 5 more minutes or until tender. Remove the peaches with a slotted spoon, and cover with plastic wrap and allow to cool. Meanwhile, turn the fire up to high, and bring the wine mixture to a boil, reducing to about 3 ounces. Discard vanilla bean and allow the wine sauce to cool. Arrnage two peach halves on each dessert plate, and drizzle the wine sauce over the peaches. Garnish with mint, and serve with vanilla frozen yogurt, if desired.

90 calories each; 140 calories with 2 ounces of vanilla frozen yogurt.

SOUFFLÉ GRAND MARNIER

What could be more elegant to finish a good French meal than a wonderful soufflé, carried to the table with pride, all piping hot and golden brown? But, on the other hand, aren't soufflés fickle things with a devious mind of their own that never rise when you want them to, and fall in the oven if something goes thump upstairs? Well, perhaps... but how about a near fool-proof soufflé that you can make and serve with confidence...and low in calories too. Sound too good to be true? Try it and be amazed!

These are best served with Crème Anglaise--break open the middle of the soufflé at the table and ladle in some sauce--see recipe in Sauces. Even with these soufflés, remember the old adage, "A souffl waits for no man."

Serves 6

1	orange	
6	egg whites	
9	tablespoons	sugar (divided)
4	tablespoons	cornstarch
2	ounces	Grand Marnier
	butter & sugar for dusting	

Heat oven to 350°F. Boil a kettle full of water. Grate off the colored skin of the orange (the zest), taking care not to grate the white pith underneath it. Reserve the grated zest, and set the orange aside for another use (for example, Oranges à la Grand Marnier). Whip egg whites and 3 tablespoons of the sugar to form soft peaks. Mix together remaining sugar, orange zest, and cornstarch. Gently fold in the dry ingredients, then fold in the Grand Marnier. Butter 6 four ounce ramekins, then dust fully with sugar, especially the sides. Fill 3/4 or so with mixture. Arrange the ramekins in a baking pan, and place in the oven. Then pour boiling water into the pan, halfway up the sides of the ramekins. Bake 8 to 12 minutes. These are done when the tops appear to dry out (and may crack--that's okay). They are much more stable than traditional soufflés, but still must be served *immediately* or they will fall.

To make the decoration shown in the picture, simply drizzle some lines of Raspberry Coulis over a pool of Crème Anglaise. Then draw a toothpick up and back across the lines, as shown in the diagram.

151 calories each

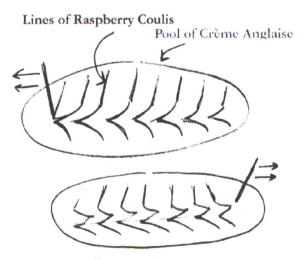

Lines of Raspberry Coulis

Pool of Crème Anglaise

Double arrows show direction of toothpick sweep

Tarte aux Fraises
STRAWBERRY TART

Serves 8

This is a marvelous low calorie dessert that looks smashing when served. It can be prepared as individual tartlets, if you prefer to avoid the challenge of cutting it before guests (incidentally, to cut a whole tart most attractively, do it in the kitchen with an electric knife). Either use the tart crust recipe and divide up the batter into tartlet molds, or use the phyllo based tartlet recipe. Instead of strawberries, it can be made with raspberries in season, or with rows of blueberries or blackberries between strawberries and raspberries. Use your imagination to artistically lay out the berries for the best appearance. It's very simple to put together, even at the last minute, if you've prepared the custard and held it in the refrigerator, and cut the fruit ahead of time. It gets soggy if prepared too far ahead, but it does hold nicely for several hours.

At the bakery in Paris: note the variety of fruit used

1   tart crust, pre-baked (see recipe for Pâte à Tarte)
1   package   vanilla pudding mix: no-sugar, no-fat
2   cups   skim milk
1   quart   strawberries, picked over and tops sliced off
     red currant jelly for glaze

Prepare the vanilla pudding mix according to package directions for "pie filling," substituting the skim milk for whatever milk is suggested. Allow to cool completely in the refrigerator. Fill center of pre-baked tart with custard. Arrange strawberries, cut side down, on the custard. Warm jelly to melting point in a small pan, adding 1 tablespoons water to thin slightly. Glaze berries using a pastry brush. Serve within 3 hours.

166 calories each slice.

Tarte aux Poires
PEAR TART

Serves 8

2	pears
1	tablespoon lemon juice
2	tablespoons sugar
1	package vanilla pudding mix--fat free, sugar free *
1 3/4	cups skim milk
1	recipe tart crust pre-baked (see recipe for Pâte à Tarte)
1	sprig mint leaves
	apricot preserves or apple jelly for glaze

*Or make up a recipe of Crème Patisserie, see Basics.

Peel and halve the pears. Using a melon baller, scoop out the seeds. Slice the pears almost but not all the way to the pointed end. Pressing down with your palm, fan out the pears. Paint the pears with a little lemon juice to prevent browning. Sprinkle them with the sugar. Spray a cookie sheet with pan spray, lay out the pears, and broil about ten minutes until a golden color appears and pears are cooked through. Prepare the vanilla custard according to the direction for "pie filling" using the skim milk. After the tart shell has cooled, fill the tart shell with the custard--you may not use it all. Lay out the fanned pear halves on the custard and decorate the center with a mint leaf sprig.

Warm the apple jelly or apricot preserves to melting point in a small pan, and thin with a tablespoon of water. Using a pastry brush, glaze the pears. Serve within 2 to 3 hours of preparation.

180 calories per serving.

Tarte Tatin
THE TATIN SISTERS' APPLE TART

This is my version of that upside-down apple tart made famous by the Tatin sisters, who ran a small hotel in France, many years ago. I tried many alternatives for the tart base, starting with home-made pastry. No way could I get the calorie count down low enough without removing all traces of good taste. Then I found a recipe that suggested toasted slices of white bread, crust removed, cut out to fit the top of the pan and painted with melted butter and sugar. A disaster! The "crust" fell apart before I could think about cutting it. I tried phyllo pastry. The pastry burns before the apples came close to cooked. I was browsing the supermarket one day, and I read the calorie count on the side of a package of refrigerator crescent rolls. The count is too high if you're just going to sit down and eat rolls, but I thought I might get just enough dough by using two rolls for the whole crust for 8 people, the count would be just fine, and I'd be starting with dough that needs to bake as long as the apples do. If the apples were sweetened enough, the fact that the dough isn't sweet might be okay...it works!

Serves 8

    1   cup sugar
    1   cup water
    1 1/2 lbs. apples -- Granny Smith are a good choice if available
                    peeled -- cored and halved, each half cut in three wedges
    1 package refrigerator crescent rolls

Preheat the oven to 375°F. Spray a 9" sautoir with pan spray (a sautoir is a straight-sided fry pan; if you don't have one use any 9" fry pan). Add the sugar and water, and stir to dissolve. Place on the stove over medium-high heat, and place the apples in concentric circles in the sugar water, cored sides up. When the mixture begins to boil, cover and lower the heat slightly. Cook 15 minutes, until the apples begin to soften, then uncover and cook a further 20 to 30 minutes until the sugar begins to caramelize. Do not overcook or the caramel will burn and you will start over. The length of cooking time depends in part on the water content of the apples. Remove from the heat, and cool slightly.

Meanwhile, remove two of the crescent rolls from the package, and press them edge to edge with your fingers on a flat work surface to form a rectangle. Reserve the other rolls for another use. Using a rolling pin, roll the dough into a circle about 9" in diameter. Place the circle of dough on top of the apples in the pan, then place the sautoir in the oven for about 10 to 15 minutes, until the top is golden brown. Remove from the oven, and allow to cool about 10 minutes. Invert carefully onto a platter. Some of the apples may stick to the pan--no matter--simply replace them and shape up the tart.

Serve warm with a 2 ounce scoop of vanilla frozen yogurt (add 55 calories), if desired.
127 calories per slice.

Tartelette du Fruit de l'Été
PHYLLO TARTLETS OF SUMMER FRUIT

Serves 4

Any leftover fruit can be spooned into a leftover crêpe with some yogurt for a nice treat for breakfast, lunch or dessert.

2		peaches -- peeled and chopped
1	pint	strawberries -- hulled, halved
1/2	pint	blueberries -- picked over
1	cup	cherries -- pitted
1		pear -- peeled & chopped
1/4	cup	orange juice
1/4	cup	Framboise (raspberry liqueur—or other liqueur as desired)
1	cup	vanilla lowfat yogurt
4		phyllo tartlette shells --see recipe
		mint leaves for garnish

Combine fruit with juice and Framboise. Allow to infuse several hours. Place 1/4 cup vanilla yogurt in each tartlette shell, and add a generous amount of fruit. Garnish with mint leaves.

207 calories per serving.

Tarte ou Frangipane aux Pêches ou aux Abricots
TART OR FRANGIPANE OF PEACHES OR APRICOTS

A frangipane is type of tart where the pastry cream is replaced with almond cream. This is essentially a master recipe for a peach tart, in which you can substitute apricots for peaches and frangipane for pastry cream, as you wish.

Serves 8
1 recipe tart crust pre-baked only halfway (see Basics)
1 recipe frangipane or crème patisserie (see Basics)
2 15 ounce cans peach halves, slices, or apricot halves
    apricot preserves for glazing

Spread a cooled tart crust with the pastry cream or frangipane, and arrange the fruit attractively on top. Bake in the top third of the oven at 375°F for about twenty minutes, then switch to broil for about five minutes until the edges of the fruit begin to brown. Let cool slightly.

Melt the apricot preserves in a non-stick sauté pan, thinning with a tablespoon of water. Using a pastry brush, glaze each fruit, and let cool. Cut the tart into 8 pieces. Serve at room temperature.

For the frangipane: 145 calories per slice for the apricot, 155 calories per slice for the peach. For the crème patisserie: 131 calories for the apricot, 141 calories for the peach.
Wouldn't this make a fabulous Saturday morning breakfast with a cup of good café au lait!

Pavés Aux Fruits
FRUIT PAVÉS

(Pa-VAYS)

Pavé means a cobblestone or paving stone, and that is the term used to describe the delightful danish-like rectangular pastries that are occasionally found at the patisserie. They are traditionally made with a base of sponge cake, layered with vanilla-flavored butter cream, or with puff pastry, fruit and glaze. This adaptation makes them low-cal enough for an everyday dessert, with tea, or as a

Ready for the oven...

great breakfast treat. Use them the day you make them--but they are so good, you won't have any trouble getting volunteers to eat them.

Makes 12 pavés

4	sheets phyllo dough
8	teaspoons sugar
12	ounces real sour cream (not light)
2	15 ounce cans apricot halves or sliced peaches, rinsed and drained
	apricot preserves for glaze

Preheat the oven to 350°F. Following directions for keeping phyllo pastry moist while working,

...and ready to eat!

lay a sheet of phyllo dough onto a non-stick cookie sheet which has been coated with pan spray. Now, spray the phyllo with pan spray, and from a height of about one and half feet, sprinkle two teaspoons of sugar evenly over it. Repeat with the remaining three sheets. Using a pair of scissors, carefully cut the stack of sheets into 12 rectangles (3x4). Place two tablespoons of sour cream in the center of each rectangle. Arrange the apricot halves or peach slices attractively on the sour cream. Bake for about 20 minutes in the upper third of the oven, then switch the oven to broil and watch carefully, removing them from the oven when the cream and phyllo begin to turn golden brown.

Allow to cool slightly while you melt about a third of a cup of apricot preserves in a small non-stick saucepan, adding about a tablespoon of water to thin the preserves slightly. You can bring the preserves to the simmering point, and then let them cool two minutes before you start the glazing. Using a pastry brush, glaze each fruit separately. If the glaze cools too much while working, simply reheat it to melt. Serve at room temperature.

103 calories each for the apricot, 99 calories each for the peach.

Index to recipes in English and French

Secrets of

The French Diet

Cuisine Française pour Rester Mince

FRENCH CUISINE TO LOSE WEIGHT

If you have enjoyed these recipes as much as I have, you will be looking forward to Volume II of *Secrets of The French Diet*. Send your name and address to the publisher below and you will be the first to know when Volume II is ready!

Already planned are such wonderful recipes as, from...

...**Lyon:** Grilled Lobster Diablotur, Chef Gerard Nandron (Le Pavillon du Parc); Milk-Fed Veal with a Crust of Morel Mushrooms, Chef Phillippe Chavent (La Tour Rose); John Dory with Fried Leeks, Chef Pierre Orsi (Pierre Orsi); and Free-Range Chicken Sautéed with a Carrot Reduction Sauce and Spinach, Chef Jean-Paul Lacombe (Léon de Lyon).

...**Le Bugue (the Dordogne):** Tuna Steak Marinated in Sea Salt, Chef Yves Scaviner (Les Trois As).

...**Perigueux:** Hangar Steak with Spring Vegetables, Chef Christian Martin (Hercule Poireau).

...**St. Barthèlemy, French West Indies:** Red Snapper with Cocoanut Milk and Red Pepper Sabayon, Chef Bruno Benedetti (François Plantation).

...**Laguiole:** Grilled Lobster with Cilantro and Confit of Orange Zest, Chef Michel Bras (Michel Bras).

Complete this only if you have bought this book at a store. Mail order clients will already be registered with us. Send us a note and tell us what you liked, or didn't, and what you want to see more of!

Name_____

Address_____

City_____State_____Zip_____

Fax No._____E-Mail_____

Mail to: Worldwide Publishing, Inc.
            P.O. Box 750
            Loris, SC 29569-0750